NEW DIRECTIONS FOR ADULT AND CONTI

D0286886

Ralph G. Brockett, *University of Tennessee, Knoxville*
EDITOR-IN-CHIEF

Alan B. Knox, *University of Wisconsin, Madison*
CONSULTING EDITOR

An Update on Adult Learning Theory

Sharan B. Merriam
University of Georgia, Athens

EDITOR

Number 57, Spring 1993

JOSSEY-BASS PUBLISHERS
San Francisco

AN UPDATE ON ADULT LEARNING THEORY
Sharan B. Merriam (ed.)
New Directions for Adult and Continuing Education, no. 57
Ralph G. Brockett, Editor-in-Chief
Alan B. Knox, Consulting Editor

Microfilm copies of issues and articles are available in 16mm and 35mm,
as well as microfiche in 105mm, through University Microfilms Inc., 300
North Zeeb Road, Ann Arbor, Michigan 48106.

LC 85-644750   ISSN 0195-2242   ISBN 1-55542-684-0

NEW DIRECTIONS FOR ADULT AND CONTINUING EDUCATION is part of The
Jossey-Bass Higher and Adult Education Series and is published quarterly
by Jossey-Bass Inc., Publishers, 350 Sansome Street, San Francisco,
California 94104-1310 (publication number USPS 493-930). Second-class
postage paid at San Francisco, California, and at additional mailing offices.
POSTMASTER: Send address changes to New Directions for Adult and
Continuing Education, Jossey-Bass Inc., Publishers, 350 Sansome Street,
San Francisco, California 94104-1310.

SUBSCRIPTIONS for 1993 cost $45.00 for individuals and $60.00 for institutions, agencies, and libraries.

EDITORIAL CORRESPONDENCE should be sent to the Editor-in-Chief, Ralph
G. Brockett, Dept. of Technological and Adult Education, University of
Tennessee, 402 Claxton Addition, Knoxville, Tennessee 37996-3400.

Cover photograph by Wernher Krutein/PHOTOVAULT © 1990.

CONTENTS

EDITOR'S NOTES

The effort of trying to understand learning in adulthood is at once fascinating and frustrating—fascinating because of the complexity of the phenomenon, frustrating because this same complexity defies simple description. Over the years a number of theories, models, or sets of principles have been proposed, each of which purports to capture the nature and the uniqueness of adult learning. However, no single explanation has emerged as a rallying point by which adult educators can define and explain just what goes on when a learner enters the classroom, apprentices himself or herself to an expert, or checks out a videotape to learn a new skill. Instead, we have a colorful mosaic with pieces yet to be filled in.

The purpose of this volume, *An Update on Adult Learning Theory,* is to stand back and assess where we are in our understanding of adult learning. The goal is to take stock of the company store, checking out the status of old standbys and assessing the potential of newer additions. Toward that end, eight of the chapters here highlight different formulations of or approaches to adult learning. The authors of these chapters were asked to present the assumptions and major tenets of their respective topics, to specify how each particular approach has contributed to our understanding of adult learning, and to assess the impact that the theory, model, or perspective has had on the practice of adult education. In the other two chapters, the first and the last, I provide a foundation for and reflect on the content presented in the rest of the volume.

In Chapter One, I trace the development of the knowledge base in adult learning, beginning with Thorndike, Bregman, Tilton, and Woodyard's (1928) *Adult Learning,* published within two years of the founding of adult education as a professional field of practice. Dependence on psychologists' study of learning behavior eventually gave way to the efforts of adult educators to articulate characteristics of *adult* learning. Finally, recent years have seen an infusion of yet other disciplines and perspectives (several of which are covered by chapters in this volume) in the understanding of learning in adulthood.

Chapters Two through Five focus on efforts by adult educators to explain adult learning and, in particular, how it might differ from the learning in which children engage. In Chapter Two, Daniel D. Pratt assesses Malcolm Knowles's andragogy after twenty-five years. Andragogy, our ambassador to the rest of education, is inarguably the best known set of principles explaining learning in adulthood, or, more accurately, characteristics of adult learners. Pratt frames his assessment of andragogy's contribution around four key questions about learning.

1

The notion of self-directed learning has received nearly equal attention within the field of adult education. In Chapter Three, Rosemary S. Caffarella delineates the basic ideas underpinning this rather confusing concept and then discusses what the relevant body of literature has contributed to our understanding of adult learning.

Roger Hiemstra, in Chapter Four, puts three other models of adult learning under the microscope, each of which has potential for illuminating aspects of adult learning but has yet to receive much attention. These models are Cross's Chain of Response and Characteristics of Adults as Learners, Knox's proficiency theory, and McCluskey's theory of margin.

Transformational learning, especially as conceptualized by Jack Mezirow, is yet another attempt by adult educators to identify what is unique about adult learning. Currently, Mezirow's theory of perspective transformation is undergoing the same scrutiny and debate that andragogy underwent in the 1970s. M. Carolyn Clark gives us a status report on this perspective in Chapter Five.

The next four chapters represent other perspectives that have found advocates and expression in adult education. Each of these four perspectives has something to add to our understanding of adult learning. In Chapter Six, Marcie Boucouvalas reviews the vast and scattered literature on consciousness and learning that helps us to understand learning that is more intuitive, dialectic, and transpersonal.

In contrast to Boucouvalas's focus on internal consciousness, Arthur L. Wilson, in Chapter Seven, highlights situated cognition. The unifying theme of this approach is that knowing and learning can only be understood within the social world or context in which they occur. Donald Schön's work on reflection-in-action and knowing-in-action is a key component of this perspective.

In Chapter Eight, Michael R. Welton does a yeoman's job in explaining critical theory, one of the more intriguing but also more difficult perspectives that has recently found its way into the literature and discussions of the field. The major contribution of this approach has been a critique of the practice of adult education and the assumptions underlying much of what we presume to know about adult learning.

The final perspective presented is feminist pedagogy. Elizabeth J. Tisdell, in Chapter Nine, explains how this approach sensitizes us to the struggle of women to become empowered collectively and individually, how this struggle plays out in adult learning situations, and how it affects the nature of women's learning and knowing.

In Chapter Ten, I summarize the ideas and perspectives discussed in the previous chapters. My aim is to assess where we are today in our understanding of adult learning—a status report containing speculations about future directions for filling in even more of the pieces in the mosaic of adult learning.

Sharan B. Merriam
Editor

Reference

Thorndike, E. L., Bregman, E. O., Tilton, J. W., and Woodyard, E. *Adult Learning.* New York: Macmillan, 1928.

SHARAN B. MERRIAM is professor of adult education at the University of Georgia, Athens, and coeditor of Adult Education Quarterly.

Early efforts to understand how adults learn were by psychologists who studied learning in general; adult educators then joined in. Recently, other perspectives have been developed to help us understand adult learning.

Adult Learning: Where Have We Come from? Where Are We Headed?

Sharan B. Merriam

The question is inevitable. I can sense it coming. It arises in casual conversation with the person in an adjacent seat on the airplane, at a meeting with a colleague from another department, in conversation with a new acquaintance at a social event. It is the question about what I do, what I teach, what my "area" is. I have experimented with various answers ranging from the simple "adult education" (hoping that this answer will have the same effect as saying "biology" or "history") to the "more-than-you-ever-wanted-to-know"-type answers. Once, I even tried out a response that one of my colleagues uses—"adult psychology"—but I felt like a traitor and have not used it since. My best response is to follow "adult education" with a statement about my interest in better understanding how adults learn, what they are interested in learning, where they learn, and so on. This response does not shorten the process of explanation, but eventually most people can identify some learning that they have done as adults. Indeed, adult learning is the "glue" holding together a field that is diverse in content, clientele, and delivery systems.

We actually know quite a bit about adult learning. We know who is most likely to participate in formal learning activities, why they do, and when and where this learning is likely to take place. We also know something of the informal, often self-initiated and self-planned learning projects that most adults have going on at any particular point in time. Finally, we know a bit about how this learning takes place, that is, the process of acquiring, processing, and utilizing new knowledge. It is the *how* of adult learning that is the focus of this volume.

Much of what we know about how learning takes place draws from

New Directions for Adult and Continuing Education, no. 57, Spring 1993 © Jossey-Bass Publishers

work conducted in the first half of this century by educational psychologists and somewhat later by developmental psychologists. As adult education became more clearly defined as a field of practice and study, efforts were directed toward determining what, if anything, is unique about learning in adulthood. Recently, writings and research from other disciplines have helped to illuminate adult learning. In this chapter, I trace these various contributions to our understanding of adult learning, thereby providing a backdrop for the in-depth and up-to-date analyses of recent developments in adult learning presented in subsequent chapters.

Can Adults Learn?

For centuries, people have known that learning and living are so intricately intertwined that one cannot be separated from the other. However, somewhere along the line, learning became so strongly associated with formal educational activities that it takes considerable probing for an adult to identify learning apart from "taking a class." This institutionalization of learning has led us to question the adult's capacity to learn and whether or not intelligence declines with age. Much of the early work in adult learning focused on questions such as these.

Thorndike, Bregman, Tilton, and Woodyard's (1928) book, *Adult Learning,* represented the first systematic investigations of adult learning. By testing people between fourteen and fifty years of age on various memory and learning tasks, these psychologists concluded that "teachers of adults of age twenty-five to forty-five should expect them to learn at nearly the same rate and in nearly the same manner as they would have learned the same thing at twenty" (1928, pp. 178–179). They constructed a learning curve, suggesting that the rate of learning declines 1 percent per year between ages twenty-five and fifty. Other research on adult intelligence in the 1930s also found a decline, but one beginning at a later age and not as sharp as Thorndike, Bregman, Tilton, and Woodyard's curve (Jones and Conrad, 1933; Miles and Miles, 1932).

Findings from much of this early research were a function of research design; that is, tests of older adults against young people under timed conditions made it appear that young adults were better learners. Lorge (1944, 1947) later pointed out that adult test scores were related to previous education and skills, not to age per se. Since older adults had less formal education and less opportunity to develop test-taking skills, it only appeared that they were less capable learners. Moreover, when Lorge focused on power, or ability to learn, rather than on the speed or rate of learning (that is, when time pressure was removed), adults up to age seventy did as well as younger adults.

The concept of intelligence and, subsequently, its measurement also became more complex. Wechsler (1958), who developed an instrument

(Adult Intelligence Scale) to measure adult intelligence that is still in use today, noted that declines occurred on some subtests but not on others. Since the 1960s, a number of multifactor models of intelligence have been proposed and tested. Among the most prominent are Cattell's (1963, 1987) theory of fluid and crystallized intelligence, Guilford's (1967) structure of intellect, Gardner's (1983) theory of multiple intelligences, and Sternberg's (1985) triarchic theory. Typically, adults score better on some aspects of intelligence as they age, and worse on others, resulting in a fairly stable composite measure of intelligence until very old age (Schaie and Willis, 1986).

In addition to intelligence, other aspects of human learning have occupied educational psychologists, gerontologists, and developmental psychologists for most of the past fifty years. When adults are the focus of this research, most of the investigations are framed in terms of chronological age. That is, researchers investigate how advancing age influences the ability to remember, to process information, and to problem solve. Generalizations from this set of literature are difficult to make. Much of the research has been conducted in laboratories or other artificial settings, making its applicability to real-life situations questionable. Further, deficits and declines are often shown to be functions of noncognitive factors such as level of education, training, health, and speed of response (Merriam and Caffarella, 1991).

Researchers have also been interested in delineating stages of cognitive development, some of which focus on adulthood. Arlin (1975), for example, suggested that there is a fifth stage of problem finding that follows Piaget's four stages of cognitive development (the fourth being formal operations and problem solving in the teenage years). Perry (1981) proposed stages based on data from young adult college students, and Belenky, Clinchy, Goldberger, and Tarule (1986) grouped women's ways of knowing into five major categories. Proponents of yet another way of conceptualizing cognitive development have suggested that mature thought entails the ability to accept inherent contradictions and ambiguities, a dialectic process (Basseches, 1984; Pascual-Leone, 1983; Riegel, 1973). Much of the work on cognitive development is theoretical and is subject to some of the same criticisms directed at other age and stage models of personality, ego, and moral development.

The latest concerns of some educational, cognitive, and developmental psychologists, which holds the most promise for our understanding of learning in adulthood, involve consideration of experience, personal history, and social and cultural contexts. How is it, for example, that adults in a laboratory cannot memorize nonsense syllables as well as young people but yet are able to remember enormous blocks of technical information related to their jobs? Or they cannot solve simple mathematics problems in a paper-and-pencil test but can figure out how many grams of a particular food are allowed in a special diet? Or they cannot identify the implied meaning of a reading passage but can advise another person on a complex personal problem? Even wisdom, considered by many to be the pinnacle of cognitive development, is experientially defined and culturally bound (Sternberg, 1990).

So, adults can learn, and depending on how learning is measured and assessed, they can learn as well as young people. From Thorndike onward, psychologists have systematically investigated human learning behavior. The emphasis with regard to adults has been on the changes in learning, memory, intelligence, and cognition that occur as adults age, although some recent thinking has broadened the focus to include considerations of context and life experience (see Merriam and Caffarella, 1991; Tennant, 1988).

What Is Different About Adult Learning?

For a while, it seems, adult educators were satisfied with the practice of drawing on the research in psychology for an understanding of learning. But as part of the drive to differentiate their profession as a separate field of practice from other forms of education, adult educators began to consider whether adult learning could be distinguished from learning in childhood. Attempts at codifying these differences as a set of principles, a model, or even a theory of adult learning have been, and continue to be, pursued by adult educators. Three of the most prominent efforts are discussed here.

Approximately twenty-five years ago, Malcolm Knowles introduced the European concept of andragogy to North American adult educators. Andragogy, "the art and science of helping adults learn," was contrasted with pedagogy, the art and science of helping children learn (Knowles, 1980, p. 43). Andragogy became a rallying point for those trying to define the field of adult education as separate from other areas of education. However, close scrutiny of the five assumptions and their implications for practice by educators in and out of adult education led Knowles to back off his original stance that andragogy characterized only adult learning. The clearest indication of this rethinking is the change in the subtitles of the 1970 and 1980 editions of *The Modern Practice of Adult Education*. The 1970 subtitle is *Andragogy Versus Pedagogy*, whereas the 1980 subtitle is *From Pedagogy to Andragogy*. Knowles's later position, as reflected in the 1980 subtitle, is that pedagogy-andragogy represents a continuum ranging from teacher-directed to student-directed learning and that both approaches are appropriate with children and adults depending on the situation. For example, adults who know little or nothing about a topic benefit from teacher-directed instruction until they have enough knowledge to begin directing their own learning. Thus, while andragogy does not define the uniqueness of adult learning, it does provide a set of guidelines for designing instruction with learners who are more self-directed than teacher-directed.

A second major thrust in distinguishing adult learning from childhood learning is derived from Houle's (1961), Tough's ([1971] 1979), and Knowles's (1975) early work on what has come to be known as self-directed learning. Grounded in the notion that adults are independent and thus self-directing, this line of inquiry is almost exclusively adult-oriented. Tough's original research uncovered the fact that nearly 90 percent of adults are engaged in learning projects, 70 percent of which are planned by the learners.

Research and theory-building efforts in self-directed learning focused, first, on documenting its existence and then delineating its characteristics. Specifically, the emphasis has been on identifying resources used by learners, the quality of the learning, the competencies needed to engage in this type of learning, whether self-directedness is a personality character-istic, and the conceptual meaning of the term *self-directed learning* (Merriam and Caffarella, 1991). There has been no research to date aimed at establishing whether self-directed learning is a uniquely *adult* undertaking, or whether the *process* of learning in this manner is uniquely adult. However, this body of literature has helped to define learning in adulthood.

A third major thrust in distinguishing adult education from preadult education is illustrated by Mezirow's theory of perspective transformation. In numerous writings, Mezirow has developed a theory that explains how adult learning is different from learning in childhood. According to Mezirow (1990, p. 14), the hallmark of adult learning is "becoming critically aware of how and why our presuppositions have come to constrain the way we perceive, understand, and feel about our world; of reformulating these assumptions to permit a more inclusive, discriminating, permeable, and integrative perspective, and of making decisions or otherwise acting upon these new understandings. *More inclusive, discriminating, permeable, and integrative perspectives are superior perspectives* that adults choose if they can because they are motivated to better understand the meaning of their existence." Critical reflection and awareness of "*why* we attach the mean-ings we do to reality . . . may be the most significant distinguishing characteristics of adult learning" (Mezirow, 1981, p. 11).

Just as andragogy stimulated a great deal of debate as the field wrestled with the problem of distinguishing adult learners from children, so too Mezirow's theory of perspective transformation has generated contro-versy. In addition to issues stemming from the philosophical underpin-nings of Mezirow's theory, it is not at all clear whether perspective transformations are limited to adulthood, whether they are common occurrences, and what the specific cognitive and affective dimensions of the process are. As the scrutiny and debate continue, it is not yet clear whether perspective transformation will emerge as a unifying concept distinguishing adult from child learning.

While andragogy, self-directed learning, and perspective transformation define three major attempts at distinguishing adult learning, there are several other, lesser-known models and formulations, each of which has contributed to our understanding of learning in adulthood. McClusky's (1970) theory of margin speaks to an adult's life situation in which a ratio of "load" to "power" (resources needed to counter the load) results in a margin in life that is necessary to engage in learning. Knox's (1980) proficiency theory posits that adult learning is motivated by a discrepancy between current and desired levels of proficiency. Jarvis's (1987) model, which maps out nine possible responses to a life experience, is based on research with adults but does not claim to uniquely characterize adults. Finally, Cross's (1981) Characteristics of Adults as Learners model, while offering a "framework for thinking about *what* and *how* adults learn" (p. 248), has yet to be applied or tested.

Certainly, efforts by adult educators to define what is unique about learning in adulthood will continue to engage researchers and practitioners alike. Meanwhile, some adult educators are turning their attention to developments outside the field of adult education for help in understanding adult learning.

In What Other Ways Can We Understand Adult Learning?

In addition to developing the knowledge base from within, historically, adult educators have borrowed from other disciplines to inform their practice. As reviewed in the first part of this chapter, psychology has been drawn on to shed light on learning in general, and on learning and aging in adulthood in particular. Adult educators continue to utilize the work of cognitive, developmental, and educational psychologists; so too, adult educators continue to try to articulate the differences between adult and child learning. Along with these two thrusts, though, is the infusion into adult education of other perspectives represented in other bodies of literature. Three such perspectives have received prominence in recent years: sociology, critical theory, and feminist pedagogy. Since these perspectives are covered in chapters in this volume, they are reviewed only briefly here.

As noted, North American adult education has been dominated by a psychological perspective, that is, the concerns, issues, and characteristics of the individual adult have come to frame our research and our practice. However, adult education in other parts of the world (and during the 1940s in North America) has tended to place the field within a larger sociocultural perspective. This perspective has implications for better understanding the learning of adults. As Jarvis (1987, p. 11) observed, "Learning is not just a psychological process that happens in splendid isolation from the world in which the learner lives, but is intimately related to that world and affected by it." What adults apparently "choose" to learn, their access to learning opportunities, and, indeed, how they go about the learning process may be as much a function of the sociocultural environment as individual mental processes. For example, a return to school to make a career change is much more of a possibility for middle- and upper-middle-class adults than for working-class adults. Social class "shapes the choices, opportunities, and obstacles an adult is likely to face, as well as the way in which those choices and obstacles are met" (Bee, 1987, p. 51).

How society is structured also plays a role in determining who has access to various opportunities. Thus, continuing education for professional groups, for example, looks quite a bit different in setting and sponsorship from on-the-job training for blue-collar workers. Social norms and social structure influence how learning proceeds. Some cultural groups, for example, prefer to learn in a collaborative rather than individual format, as evidenced by learning style instruments that measure factors such as greater field dependence versus independence (Brookfield, 1986). As yet another example of the influence of social structure on learning, Spear and Mocker (1984, p. 4) found that adults with less than a high school education do not preplan their learning projects but rather structure them via the "limited alternatives which happen to occur in their environment." They call this phenomenon the "organizing circumstance." Finally, proponents of the growing body of literature on "situated cognition" maintain that it is only possible to really understand learning from the perspective of the social world in which it occurs.

Proponents of critical theory (also known as critical social theory) also focus on the social context in which adult education and adult learning take place. Their objective, however, is to uncover oppressive forces that hinder individuals from developing their full potential. At the same time, critical theorists are interested in finding ways to empower people individually and collectively to change the oppressive conditions of their lives.

The major thrust of critical theory has been to critique the modern practice of adult education. A central criticism is that adult education is preoccupied with technical concerns at the expense of democratic social action. Critical theory's influence on adult learning per se has been felt largely in the literature on transformative or emancipatory learning. Freire's (1970) theory of conscientization is based on identification of forms of oppression, critical awareness of how social forces shape one's life, and action to change an oppressive reality into a liberating one. In an even more direct way, Mezirow's (1990) theory of perspective transformation, discussed above, is philosophically grounded in the writings of German critical theorist Jürgen Habermas. Mezirow draws on Habermas's areas of cognitive interest to differentiate types of learning: technical, which is task-oriented; practical or dialogic, which involves social interaction; and emancipatory, characterized by self-reflection. Mezirow equates the emancipatory type of learning with perspective transformation.

Feminist scholarship, which includes a wide range of views, is the third perspective that has recently informed adult education. There is at once a sociological, psychological, and critical dimension to this perspective. Some proponents emphasize the nature of power relations in society that result in women being an oppressed and marginalized group. Others focus on the empowerment process for the individual woman. Both orientations require a critical stance in assessing women's experience at either the societal or the individual level. Most directly relevant to a better understanding of adult learning is the work by those who consider how women's learning needs are different from those of men, how the learning environment can be structured to foster women's learning, and how women come to know and to be empowered through learning (Belenky, Clinchy, Goldberger, and Tarule, 1986; Collard and Stalker, 1991; Hayes, 1989).

In summary, these three perspectives—sociocultural, critical theory, feminist pedagogy—are being utilized by adult educators to understand more about adult learning. All three serve to widen the lens of inquiry to include considerations of the context in which the adult exists and how those contextual factors affect learning.

Where Are We Headed?

It is doubtful that a phenomenon as complex as adult learning will ever be explained by a single theory, model, or set of principles. Instead, we have a case of the proverbial elephant being described differently depending on who is talking and on which part of the animal is examined. In the first half of this century, psychologists took the lead in explaining learning behavior; from the 1960s onward, adult educators began formulating their own ideas about adult learning and, in particular, about how it might differ from learning in childhood. Both of these approaches are still operative. Currently, adult learning (along with adult education as a whole) is being examined from perspectives outside the field.

Each effort contributes to our understanding of learning in adulthood. Where we are headed, it seems, is toward a multifaceted understanding of adult learning, reflecting the inherent richness and complexity of the phenomenon. The chapters that follow document and evaluate the contribution of various approaches to understanding the whole of adult learning.

References

Arlin, P. K. "Cognitive Development in Adulthood: A Fifth Stage?" *Developmental Psychology*, 1975, *11*, 602–606.

Basseches, M. *Dialectical Thinking and Adult Development.* Norwood, N.J.: Ablex, 1984.

Bee, H. L. *The Journey of Adulthood.* New York: Macmillan, 1987.

Belenky, M. F., Clinchy, B. M., Goldberger, N. R., and Tarule, J. M. *Women's Ways of Knowing: The Development of Self, Voice, and Mind.* New York: Basic Books, 1986.

Brookfield, S. D. *Understanding and Facilitating Adult Learning: A Comprehensive Analysis of Principles and Effective Practices.* San Francisco: Jossey-Bass, 1986.

Cattell, R. B. "Theory of Fluid and Crystallized Intelligence: A Critical Approach." *Journal of Educational Psychology,* 1963, *54* (1), 1–22.

Cattell, R. B. *Intelligence: Its Structure, Growth, and Action.* Amsterdam, The Netherlands: North-Holland, 1987.

Collard, S., and Stalker, J. "Women's Trouble: Women, Gender, and the Learning Environment." In R. Hiemstra (ed.), *Creating Environments for Effective Adult Learning.* New Directions for Adult and Continuing Education, no. 50. San Francisco: Jossey-Bass, 1991.

Cross, K. P. *Adults as Learners: Increasing Participation and Facilitating Learning.* San Francisco: Jossey-Bass, 1981.

Freire, P. *Pedagogy of the Oppressed.* New York: Seabury, 1970.

Gardner, H. *Frames of Mind.* New York: Basic Books, 1983.

Guilford, J. P. *The Nature of Human Intelligence.* New York: McGraw-Hill, 1967.

Hayes, E. R. "Insights from Women's Experiences for Teaching and Learning." In E. R. Hayes (ed.), *Effective Teaching Styles.* New Directions for Adult and Continuing Education, no. 43. San Francisco: Jossey-Bass, 1989.

Houle, C. O. *The Inquiring Mind.* Madison: University of Wisconsin Press, 1961.

Jarvis, P. *Adult Learning in the Social Context.* London: Croom-Helm, 1987.

Jones, H. E., and Conrad, H. S. "The Growth and Decline of Intelligence." *Genetic Psychology Monographs,* 1933, *13,* 223–298.

Knowles, M. S. *Self-Directed Learning.* New York: Association Press, 1975.

Knowles, M. S. *The Modern Practice of Adult Education: From Pedagogy to Andragogy.* (2nd ed.) New York: Cambridge Books, 1980.

Knox, A. B. "Proficiency Theory of Adult Learning." *Contemporary Educational Psychology,* 1980, *5,* 378–404.

Lorge, I. "Intellectual Changes During Maturity and Old Age." *Review of Educational Research,* 1944, *14* (4), 438–443.

Lorge, I. "Intellectual Changes During Maturity and Old Age." *Review of Educational Research,* 1947, *17* (5), 326–330.

McClusky, H. S. "An Approach to a Differential Psychology of the Adult Potential." In S. M. Grabowski (ed.), *Adult Learning and Instruction.* Syracuse, N.Y.: ERIC Clearinghouse on Adult Education, 1970. (ED 045 867)

Merriam, S. B., and Caffarella, R. S. *Learning in Adulthood: A Comprehensive Guide.* San Francisco: Jossey-Bass, 1991.

Mezirow, J. D. "A Critical Theory of Adult Learning and Education." *Adult Education Quarterly,* 1981, *32* (1), 3–24.

Mezirow, J. "How Critical Reflection Triggers Transformative Learning." In J. Mezirow and Associates, *Fostering Critical Reflection in Adulthood: A Guide to Transformative and Emancipatory Learning.* San Francisco: Jossey-Bass, 1990.

Miles, C. C., and Miles, W. R. "The Correlation of Intelligence Scores and Chronological Age from Early to Late Maturity." *American Journal of Psychology,* 1932, *44,* 44–78.

Pascual-Leone, J. "Growing into Maturity: Towards a Metasubjective Theory of Adulthood Stages." In P. B. Baltes and O. G. Brim, Jr. (eds.), *Life Span Development and Behavior.* Vol. 5. San Diego: Academic Press, 1983.

Perry, W. "Cognitive and Ethical Growth: The Making of Meaning." In A. W. Chickering and Associates, *The Modern American College: Responding to the New Realities of Diverse Students and a Changing Society.* San Francisco: Jossey-Bass, 1981.

Riegel, K. F. "Dialectic Operations: The Final Period of Cognitive Development." *Human Development,* 1973, *16,* 346–370.

Schaie, K. W., and Willis, S. L. *Adult Development and Aging.* (2nd ed.) Boston: Little, Brown, 1986.

Spear, G. E., and Mocker, D. W. "The Organizing Circumstance: Environmental Determinants in Self-Directed Learning." *Adult Education Quarterly,* 1984, *35* (1), 1–10.

Sternberg, R. J. *Beyond I.Q.: A Triarchic Theory of Human Intelligence.* New York: Cambridge University Press, 1985.

Sternberg, R. J. (ed.). *Wisdom: Its Nature, Origins, and Development.* New York: Cambridge University Press, 1990.

Tennant, M. *Psychology and Adult Learning.* New York: Routledge & Kegan Paul, 1988.

Thorndike, E. L., Bregman, E. O., Tilton, J. W., and Woodyard, E. *Adult Learning.* New York: Macmillan, 1928.

Tough, A. *The Adult's Learning Projects: A Fresh Approach to Theory and Practice in Adult Learning.* (2nd ed.) Toronto, Ontario, Canada: Ontario Institute for Studies in Education, 1979. (Originally published 1971.)

Wechsler, D. *The Measure and Appraisal of Adult Intelligence.* (4th ed.) Baltimore: Williams & Wilkins, 1958.

SHARAN B. MERRIAM is professor of adult education at the University of Georgia, Athens, and coeditor of Adult Education Quarterly.

Andragogy's contribution to adult learning is examined through four questions regarding the meaning of learning, antecedents to learning, facilitation of learning, and the purposes of learning.

Andragogy After Twenty-Five Years

Daniel D. Pratt

Over the past twenty-five years, the sheer volume of articles, books, and discussion related to andragogy has been impressive, though not necessarily coherent in thematic focus or clear in defining the central concept of learning. For some, andragogy has been a prescriptive set of guidelines for the education of adults. For others, it represents a philosophical position vis-à-vis the existential nature of adults. For still others, it is an ideology based on beliefs regarding individual freedom, the relationship between individual and society, and the aims of adult education.

Throughout all of this examination, the enduring voice of Malcolm Knowles is remarkably clear and present. Amidst debate, clarification, challenge, refutation, and articulation, his message not only has persisted but is the voice most associated with andragogy in North America. Some have suggested that he endures because he speaks to people's experience, articulating a recognizable reality. Whatever the case, there is no denying that his place in the history of adult education is both secure and significant because of his promotion of andragogy.

The purpose of this chapter is to ask one central question: What contribution has andragogy made to our understanding of adult learning? In order to assess this contribution, the question is distilled into four subordinate questions that have framed the twenty-five year debate: (1) *What is learning?* Do we know any more about learning after nearly twenty-five years of discussion and debate? What does learning mean, from an andragogical perspective? (2) *What are the antecedents to adult learning?* This is a question about the relative influence of human agency versus social structures on adult learning. Where does andragogy stand in this debate? (3) *How can we facilitate adult learning?* The central issue here is freedom versus authority. How are the tensions between freedom and authority dealt with in andragogical methods and relationships? (4) *What are the aims of adult learning?* On what basis are andragogical methods and perspectives on learning justified? Should adult education seek the transformation of the individual or society?

What Is Learning?

Many adult educators in North America have either assumed or hoped that andragogy would be the basis for a theory of adult learning. As recently as 1989, Knowles alluded to his own "comprehensive theory of adult learning" as expressed in his writings on andragogy (Carlson, 1989). Yet, as prevalent as that hope is, there has been virtually no attempt to clarify the central concept of learning. Consequently, much of the discussion here regarding antecedents to learning, means of facilitating learning, and aims of adult education is intimately linked to this concept and the lack of clarity owing to its neglect. The philosophical, theoretical, and empirical claims to truth regarding the characteristics of adults as learners and the means to facilitate adult learning are dependent on the concept of learning. Without a clarification of that concept, it is doubtful that we can agree on much of what follows.

During the 1950s and 1960s in the United States, behaviorism and empiricism dominated our views on learning. From this joint perspective, it was assumed that the world existed independently of the learner or knower. To know something was to know its essence or nature. Learning was the objective perception of the world as it is, unmediated by personal interpretation or distortion. Learning that was not observable was either inaccessible, untrustworthy, or insignificant. The most common definition of learning was a change in behavior. Learning and knowledge were portrayed in terms of a person looking at the world and asking how well he or she could mirror the nature or essence of the world. In other words, if the learner was active in constructing meaning and interpreting experience, knowledge and truth were compromised.

Knowles implicitly took a different perspective about the nature of learning. Although he was not the primary force behind a shift in educational thought away from behaviorism, he was the most potent adult educator to move in this direction since Lindeman. Working backward from Knowles's five assumptions about (1) self-concept, (2) prior experience, (3) readiness to learn, (4) learning orientation, and (5) motivation to learn, we can draw inferences about andragogical perspectives on learning and knowledge. First, the world may exist, but it is the individual's experience of that world that is most important to learning. Learning is not, therefore, the discovery of an independent, preexisting world outside as much as it is the construction of meaning through experience. Second, learning is more subjective than objective, with an emphasis on individual interpretation, integration, and even transformation of knowledge. There-fore, andragogy appears to rest on two implicit principles of learning: First, knowledge is assumed to be actively constructed by the learner, not passively received from the environment; and, second, learning is an interactive process of interpretation, integration, and transformation of one's experiential world.

What Are the Antecedents of Adult Learning?

The second question deals with the nature of adults as learners, particularly those aspects of the person that are assumed to influence adult learning. In this case, we have explicit statements from which to assess the message and contribution of andragogy. Indeed, Knowles's five assumptions about characteristics of adults as learners form the heart of andragogy; they are the basis from which everything else flows and may constitute the recog-nizable reality that informs many adult educators' views of the adult learner. There is no doubt that with these assumptions Knowles struck a chord of recognition and harmony with a great many adult educators, particularly English-speaking North Americans.

Just what is this portrait and how is it constructed? First, there is an emphasis on the psychological and individualistic nature of the learner with the person's self-concept, prior experience, and perceived needs as antecedents to learning. Second, each individual is assumed to be, by nature, autonomous and desiring of self-improvement, and to have the capacity to be self-directed in learning quite apart from the social struc-tures that might bear on personal characteristics, aspirations, and the learning process. (Social structures are those institutions and systems in society that produce and reproduce rules and resources that influence the communication of meaning, the exercise of power, and the legitima-tion and judgment of conduct, for example, the family, religious institu-tions, political parties, economic policies, systems of education, cultural traditions, and historical periods; see Giddens, 1984.) Third, each person is believed to be unique, and individual differences, whether arising from experience, felt needs, or genetic nature, are to be respected and nur-tured as individuals move toward self-fulfillment. Thus, we are presented with a portrait of adult learners largely separate from their cultural and historical contexts, capable of controlling and directing their learning, and expected to develop according to their own idiosyncratic paths or potential.

In turn, what is left out and with what consequences? On the surface, it may seem to be the familiar debate about the characteristics of the adult as learner. Yet, it is also a more profound debate about what adults bring to the existential moment of learning, consciously and unconsciously, willingly and unwillingly, and how that influences learning. As Mezirow

(1981, p. 20) argues, social structures form the basis for our "conceptual categories, rules, tactics, and criteria for judging implicit habits of perception, thought, and behavior."

This is the focus of one strand of the debate on andragogy, often characterized as a debate between psychological and sociological perspectives on the nature of adults as learners (for example, Collins, 1992; Podeschi and Pearson, 1986). It is also, in essence, a debate between human agency and social structures as significant antecedents of adult learning. Clearly, andragogy comes down on the side of human agency, describing the individual in psychological terms, separate from social, political, economic, cultural, and historical contexts. As Podeschi (1987b) puts it, instead of viewing individualism as Maslow did, with the self socially situated as part of a larger whole, andragogy "has the self as the primary reality, not only as the center of volition but as the target of life."

Andragogy's view of the learner, operating as if he or she has risen above the web of social structures, only superficially acknowledges those structures by calling our attention to experience and identity. It does not acknowledge the vast influence of these structures on the formation of the person's identity and ways of interpreting the world, much of which is received and accepted without conscious consideration or reflection. In this sense, the learner is portrayed as an uncritical and unwitting member of institutions and structures that generate rules about meaning, dominance, and judgment in society. From this point of view, it is inconceivable that adults could be in control of matters of which they are unaware, for example, the cultural and historical rules and schemas about self and society that are deeply embedded within consciousness and only rarely surface for critical examination. The messages that we receive while growing up and that bombard us daily through the popular media and other social structures are assimilated uncritically into our consciousness. To suggest, therefore, that adults stand apart from society as they construct meaning is, for some, to misrepresent a significant aspect of the person and the realities that engulf adults as learners.

Thus, while andragogy posits the individual at the interpretive center of learning and cognition, many adult educators now believe that there is a reciprocal relationship between the individual and social structures—each giving meaning and shape to the other. This perspective takes us beyond Knowles's assumptions to a recognition that learning and cognition are fundamentally situated within, and related to, social and historical contexts.

How Can We Facilitate Adult Learning?

For many, andragogy is a set of procedures and practices that constitutes a distinctive form of education, in contrast to pedagogy, and most suited to adults because it acknowledges their needs, experience, and self-directed nature. This methodology of andragogy has attracted an enormous following in North America and virtually around the world. Andragogical methods or approaches have been applied in formal as well as nonformal education settings. In this sense, andragogy has become a technology of instruction or facilitation of learning, transported from one culture to another and across various settings for a multitude of purposes (for example, Diflo, 1982; Knowles, 1986; Potvin, 1975; Roy-Poirier, 1986).

It is here that much of the "gospel according to Knowles" has been uncritically adopted as technique, leaving behind the underlying purposes and ideology that buttressed the initial conception of this technique. Knowles (1984, pp. 15–18) calls this an "andragogical process design," which includes seven elements: (1) climate setting, (2) involving learners in mutual planning, (3) involving participants in diagnosing their own needs for learning, (4) involving learners in formulating their learning objectives, (5) involving learners in designing learning plans, (6) helping learners carry out their learning plans, and (7) involving learners in evaluating their learning.

A cursory reading of these elements reveals the central tenets of choice and participation in this approach: It is important to involve learners in the process of setting their own directions and means of learning and evaluation as a way of facilitating their personal autonomy and self-direction. In this sense, self-direction has become a keystone in the arching methodology of andragogy; the needs and experience of the learner take precedence over the expertise of the instructor. Collins (1992, p. 6) calls this the "technology" of self-directed learning: "Malcolm Knowles formulated self-directed learning into a readily deployable technique that has been evoked as a guiding principle and widely applied throughout the field of adult education. . . . *Self-Directed Learning: A Guide for Learners and Teachers* is a how-to text which embraces without question an ideology of technique. It describes self-directed learning and then sets out, in formulaic terms, how it has to be done, directed self-directed learning, so to speak. Those practitioners who sense that the text is not sufficiently formulaic will find reassurance in Knowles's most recent book, *Using Learning Contracts*."

Yet, while much of the attention has been on the methodology of andragogy, there is, within Knowles's writing, another consistent and significant message about relationship, the suggestion that the essence of facilitation lies not in one's approach as much as in the relationship that exists between learner and facilitator. He emphasizes this point throughout his writing when he says that andragogical approaches require a psychological climate of mutual respect, collaboration, trust, support, openness, authenticity, pleasure, and humane treatment, and that it is the responsibility of a facilitator "to provide a caring, accepting, respecting, helping social atmosphere" (Knowles, 1984, p. 17).

Implied within these words is a form of relationship that is, above all, respectful of the individual's freedom from authority and control that might inhibit the natural tendencies of growth and development. This emphasis on the nature of the relationship between learner and instructor (facilitator) is clearly connected to his assumptions regarding the nature of the adult learner and his attempt to address the existential balance between freedom and authority (Podeschi and Pearson, 1986). In this sense, it also begs the question of whether such a relationship can or should take precedence over situational factors in the exercise of individual freedom and control over instructional processes, particularly the evaluation of learning. This issue too has been a part of the debate (for example, Delahaye, 1987; Grow, 1991; Pratt, 1988).

Thus, what lies beneath andragogical guidelines for facilitating learning is more than simply a process design cum technology of instruction. Indeed, it may be the emphasis on methodology to the exclusion of relationship that has produced such mixed results in the efforts to empirically test Knowles's process design (Beder and Carrea, 1988; Conti, 1985).

What Are the Purposes and Aims of Adult Learning?

This may be the most crucial of the four questions because its purpose is to clarify the essential beliefs and values that legitimate other claims regarding the meaning of learning, antecedents to learning, and means to facilitate learning. As is often the case, the values and beliefs that buttress andragogy lie beneath the surface and must be extracted by careful analysis. In this section, I rely heavily on the work of Podeschi (1987a, 1987b, 1991) and Carlson (1989), who have consistently and thoroughly probed the philosophical roots of andragogy.

Knowles's conception of andragogy is based, in part, on beliefs about human nature, the relationship between individual and society, and a commitment to a democratic society. As early as 1950, there is evidence of these values when he says that "in adult education 'the customer is always right' in so far as his desires are compatible with the objectives of our society. Under no other assumption is democratic adult education possible, for in a democracy responsibility rests with each individual to decide the course of his own growth" (Knowles, 1950, p. 11). He is consistent and clear in his commitment to individual needs and interests as a means toward achieving a more democratic society. This same theme is expressed yet again in *The Modern Practice of Adult Education: From Pedagogy to Andragogy* (Knowles, 1980), as his writing became more prescriptive, pretentious, and even presumptuous but no less focused on the ideals of a democratic citizenship and the belief that civic and democratic virtue would arise out of natural self-fulfillment through adult education (Carlson, 1989). Consistently, he has proclaimed an ideology of middle-class America with an emphasis on self-reliance and self-fulfillment in which private interests overshadow public ends (Podeschi, 1991). Knowles's andragogy has never offered a challenge to hierarchical or exploitative structures in society. Indeed, the freedom of learners from external control, a fundamental tenet of American democracy, is seen to be contingent on the compatibility of learners' needs with the objectives of society (Carlson, 1989).

Thus, andragogy appears to be based on at least five fundamental values or beliefs: (1) a moral axiom that places the individual at the center of education and relegates the collective to the periphery, (2) a belief in the goodness of each individual and the need to release and trust that goodness, (3) a belief that learning should result in growth toward the realization of one's potential, (4) a belief that autonomy and self-direction are the signposts of adulthood within a democratic society, and (5) a belief in the potency of the individual in the face of social, political, cultural, and historical forces to achieve self-direction and fulfillment. Collectively, these beliefs constitute a particular worldview that legitimates certain forms of learning, approaches to instruction, and judgments about priorities in adult education. Clearly, andragogy is saturated with the ideals of individualism and entrepreneurial democracy. Societal change may be a by-product of individual change, but it is not a primary goal of andragogy.

Andragogy's Contribution to
Our Understanding of Learning

Andragogy has been adopted by legions of adult educators around the world and has influenced the practice of adult education across an impressive range of settings. Very likely, it will continue to be the window through which adult educators take their first look into the world of adult education. As such, the "recognizable reality" that reflected back to so many in the past twenty-five years will continue to offer familiar and recognizable ground on which to conduct adult education. From this point of view, andragogy has made an enormous contribution to adult education.

However, in terms of the original question, andragogy's contribution to our understanding of adult learning is not as grand in substance as it is in scale. The widespread and uncritical adoption of a particular view of adults as learners should not be the only measure by which we assess andragogy's contribution. From one perspective, the legions of adult educators who ascribe to andragogy may have a better understanding of adults as learners; from another perspective, that understanding may be severely limited and even distorted. Further, while andragogy may have contributed to our understanding of adults as learners, it has done little to expand or clarify our understanding of the process of learning. We cannot say, with any confidence, that andragogy has been tested and found to be, as so many have hoped, either the basis for a theory of adult learning or a unifying concept for adult education.

This limitation is not surprising when we examine the debate through the preceding four questions. Andragogy is seen to be not so much an explanatory theory about adult learning as a philosophical stance with regard to the purposes of adult education and the relationship of the individual to society. As Freire (1985, pp. 43–44) has noted, we cannot separate practice from philosophy: "All educational practice implies a theoretical stance on the educator's part. This stance in turn implies— sometimes more, sometimes less explicitly—an interpretation of (human- ity) and the world. It could not be otherwise. . . . The critical analyst will discover, in the methods and texts used by educators and students, practical value options that betray a philosophy, . . . well or poorly outlined, coherent or incoherent."

Collectively, the four questions highlight two persistent tensions that are likely to characterize further debate about andragogy. First, there is a tension between freedom and authority, especially regarding the manage- ment and evaluation of learning. Andragogy leans heavily toward learner freedom (versus teacher authority) on this issue, promoting self-direction and personal autonomy. Second, there is a tension between human agency and social structures as the most potent influences on adult learning. Here, andragogy is unconditionally on the side of human agency and the power of the individual to shed the shackles of history and circumstance in pursuit of learning. The persistence and pervasiveness of these two ten- sions explain why the discussion has moved back and forth across philo- sophical boundaries, only to return to familiar arguments and conclusions. As Podeschi (1987a, p. 14) has observed, "Empirical research cannot resolve philosophical questions, nor dissolve the philosophical assump- tions of the researcher." As long as the debate is fractured along philosophi- cal lines, there can be little hope for agreement as to definitions, antecedents, means, and aims of adult learning.

If nothing else, the past twenty-five years of discussion on andragogy confirms the idea that there can be no values-neutral position with regards to adult learning and facilitation. What too often has been missing is a clarification of underlying values and beliefs and of the central concept of learning. As a result, the debate seems at times to have taken one step forward and two backward. Therefore, as we continue to analyze and discuss andragogy, we should guard against the hegemony of representing our own interests and values as universals, whether in terms of definitions of learning, antecedents to learning, means of facilitating learning, or ideals for society. This may be the most serious challenge to the ongoing debate, especially if we wish to include adult educators from both inside and outside North America whose values are not precisely those of andragogy.

References

Beder, H., and Carrea, N. "The Effects of Andragogical Teacher Training on Adult Students' Attendance and Evaluation of Their Teachers." *Adult Education Quarterly*, 1988, *38* (2), 75– 87.

Carlson, R. "Malcolm Knowles: Apostle of Andragogy." *Vitae Scholasticae*, 1989, *8* (1), 217–233.

Collins, M. "Current Trends in Adult Education: From Self-Directed Learning to Critical Theory." Paper presented at the 6th annual meeting of the Association of Process Philosophy of Education, American Philosophical Association, Louisville, Kentucky, April 1992.

Conti, G. "The Relationship Between Teaching Style and Adult Student Learning." *Adult Education Quarterly*, 1985, *35* (4), 220–228.

Delahaye, B. "The Orthogonal Relationship Between Pedagogy and Andragogy—Some Initial Findings." *Australian Journal of Adult Education*, 1987, *27* (3), 4–7.

Diflo, K. "Process and Content: The 'Andragogical' Method in Practice." *Australian Journal of Adult Education*, 1982, *22* (1), 15–20.

Freire, P. *The Politics of Education*. South Hadley, Mass.: Bergin and Garvey, 1985.

Giddens, A. *The Constitution of Society: Outline of the Theory of Structuration*. Berkeley and Los Angeles: University of California Press, 1984.

Grow, G. O. "Teaching Learners to Be Self-Directed: A Stage Approach." *Adult Education Quarterly*, 1991, *41* (3), 125–149.

Knowles, M. S. *Informal Adult Education*. New York: Association Press, 1950.

Knowles, M. S. *The Modern Practice of Adult Education: From Pedagogy to Andragogy*. (2nd ed.) New York: Cambridge Books, 1980.

Knowles, M. S. "Introduction: The Art and Science of Helping Adults Learn." In M. S. Knowles and Associates, *Andragogy in Action: Applying Modern Principles of Adult Learning*. San Francisco: Jossey-Bass, 1984.

Knowles, M. S. *Using Learning Contracts: Practical Approaches to Individualizing and Structuring Learning*. San Francisco: Jossey-Bass, 1986.

Mezirow, J. D. "A Critical Theory of Adult Learning and Education." *Adult Education*, 1981, *32* (1), 3–24.

Podeschi, R. L. "Andragogy: Proofs or Premises?" *Lifelong Learning: An Omnibus of Practice and Research*, 1987a, *11* (3), 14–16.

Podeschi, R. L. "Lindeman, Knowles, and American Individualism." Paper presented at the 28th annual meeting of Adult Education Research Conference, Laramie, Wyoming, May 1987b.

Podeschi, R. L. "Knowles and the Mid-Century Shift in Philosophy of Adult Education." Paper presented at the 32nd annual meeting of Adult Education Research Conference, Norman, Oklahoma, May-June 1991.

Podeschi, R. L., and Pearson, E. M. "Knowles and Maslow: Differences About Freedom." *Lifelong Learning: An Omnibus of Practice and Research*, 1986, *9* (7), 16–18.

Potvin, D. "An Analysis of the Andragogical Approach to the Didactics of Distance Education." *Canadian Journal of University Continuing Education*, 1975, *2* (2), 27–36.

Pratt, D. D. "Andragogy as a Relational Construct." *Adult Education Quarterly*, 1988, *38* (3), 160–181.

Roy-Poirier, J. "The Andragogical Approach in Graduate Studies: Success or Failure?" Paper presented at the 5th annual meeting of the Canadian Association for the Study of Adult Education, Vancouver, British Columbia, Canada, May-June 1986.

DANIEL D. PRATT is associate professor in the Department of Adult, Administrative, and Higher Education at the University of British Columbia, Vancouver, Canada. His research and teaching are focused on issues related to adult learning and instruction, with particular interest in cross-cultural comparisons.

Explored in this chapter are the philosophical assumptions of self-directed learning and how the study of this subject has contributed to our understanding of learning in adulthood.

Self-Directed Learning

Rosemary S. Caffarella

Of all the ideas related to learning in adulthood, the concept of self-directed learning has captured the interest of many adult educators. For some, the concept has an almost cultlike quality to the extent that self-directedness is viewed as the essence of what adult learning is all about. Is this because we, as adult learners, have felt oppressed by earlier educational experiences and are looking for a way to justify our self-assumed responsibility for our own learning? Are our own styles of learning and personality traits such that we prefer to take charge and be in control of what and how we learn and assume that other adults are similar to us? Or as educators who were taught to equate learning with formal schooling (but somehow did not believe that this definition fit well with adult learners), were we delighted when Tough (1979) and others found that many adults can and do learn primarily through their own initiative?

Regardless of why self-directed learning is important to adult educators, inquiry into the nature and processes of self-directed learning continues to grow as evidenced by the expanded number of thoughtful and insightful publications within the last few years (for example, Brockett and Hiemstra, 1991; Caffarella and O'Donnell, 1989; Candy, 1991; Confessore and Confessore, 1992; Garrison, 1992; Grow, 1991; Hammond and Collins, 1991; Long and Associates, 1992). Although we continue to haggle over the terminology used to describe this phenomenon (Brockett and Hiemstra, 1991; Gerstner, 1992), currently three principal, but distinct, ideas are incorporated into the concept of self-directed learning: a self-initiated process of learning that stresses the ability of individuals to plan and manage their own learning, an attribute or characteristic of learners with personal autonomy as its hallmark, and a way of organizing instruction in formal settings that allows for greater learner control (Brockett and Hiemstra, 1991; Caffarella and O'Donnell, 1989; Candy, 1991). Each of these ideas about self-directed learning is explored in this chapter within the framework of the philosophical assumptions of self-directed learning and how the study of self-directed learning has contributed to our understanding of learning in adulthood. In addition, observations are made about the impact and promise of our growing knowledge base in self-directed learning for informing the future study and practice of learning in adulthood.

Philosophical Assumptions Underlying Self-Directed Learning

The predominate philosophical orientation underlying self-directed learning is humanistic in nature (for example, Hiemstra, 1992; Hiemstra and Sisco, 1990; Knowles, 1975, 1980; Long, 1992; Tough, 1979). From this perspective, the focus of learning is on the individual and self-development, with learners expected to assume primary responsibility for their own learning. The process of learning, which is centered on learner need, is seen as more important than the content; therefore, when educators are involved in the learning process, their most important role is to act as facilitators or guides, as opposed to content experts (see, for example, Long, 1992; Hiemstra, 1992; Knowles, 1980).

Although humanistic philosophy has been the primary guide for much of the work on self-directed learning, at least three other philosophical perspectives have influenced our thinking about self-directed learning: progressivism, behaviorism, and critical theory (Gerstner, 1987). From the perspective of progressivism, as in humanistic philosophy as well, the learner and the learner's experience are central to the learning process, thus highlighting the notions that learners are primarily responsible for their own learning and that educators serve as guides and encouragers in the process. Learning from this stance is practical and pragmatic in nature. The pragmatic focus of most self-directed learning activities has been documented in numerous studies (Merriam and Caffarella, 1991; Tough, 1979).

The behaviorist philosophy can be detected most strongly in descriptions of how one should go about the process of self-directed learning. Several authors have advocated that learners develop plans, often in the form of learning contracts, for their self-directed learning endeavors (Hiemstra and Sisco, 1990; Knowles, 1975). These plans or learning contracts stress the importance of specifying learning objectives (and from the behaviorist perspective only behavioral objectives are acceptable), selecting appropriate techniques for achieving those objectives, and then evaluating what one has learned in terms of the objectives proposed. Consistent with this philosophy are the additional questions of accountability and quality in terms of whether self-directed learning is really a valid and useful activity (Brookfield, 1984; Caffarella and O'Donnell, 1991).

The critical perspective, which is linked in some ways to social change, one of the major tenets of the progressivism school, has recently received more emphasis in the descriptions of self-directed learning (Brookfield, 1986; Garrison, 1992; Hammond and Collins, 1991; Mezirow, 1985). This perspective focuses on bringing about change in the present social, political, and economic order through the questioning of assumptions held by learners about the world in which they live and work. This critically reflective process of learning is coupled with action directed at altering how organizations and societies in general are organized and function (for example, changes in policies and procedures, legislative changes, and role changes). Mezirow (1985) and Brookfield (1986) were among the first writers who added this critical perspective to self-directed learning. According to Brookfield (1986, pp. 58–59), "The most fully adult form of self-directed learning . . . is one in which critical reflection on the contingent aspects of reality, the exploration of alternative perspectives and meaning systems, and the alteration of personal and social circumstances are all present." Hammond and Collins (1991) operationalized this critical perspective more fully by incorporating into their model of self-directed learning notions of critical practice. They emphasize reflective thinking as a key part of each component of their model as well as include within their "analysis" component an in-depth look at the "structure and functioning of the society in which we work" (p. 77) so that learners can better understand and respond to the context that, at least in part, shapes what and how they learn.

Contributions of the Study of Self-Directed Learning to the Understanding of Learning in Adulthood

Self-directed learning has contributed to our understanding of learning by (1) identifying an important form of adult learning and providing us with insights into the process of learning, (2) challenging us to define and debate the salient characteristics of adult learners, and (3) expanding our thinking about learning in formal settings.

Form and Process of Learning. The first contribution has its roots in the work of Houle (1961), Tough (1967, 1979), and Knowles (1975, 1980), among others. Researchers, primarily replicating Tough's original study on learning projects, have verified that a significant number of adults learn a great deal outside of the control and confines of formal educational institutions (Brookfield, 1984; Caffarella and O'Donnell, 1987). Adults on their own initiative acquire job skills, gain insights into how to manage home and family, pursue personal interests and hobbies, and just learn for the sake of acquiring knowledge. Self-direction in one's learning does not necessarily mean solitary learning. Rather, often in these self-initiated learning ventures, adults seek assistance in the form of human (for example, friends, family members, and experts in the content area) and material resources (for example, books, magazines, and videotapes). They may even choose to attend a self-help group, a course or workshop, a lecture, or some other type of formal education program as part of their self-directed learning efforts. What differentiates self-directed learning from learning in more traditional formal settings is that *the learner chooses to assume the primary responsibility for planning, carrying out, and evaluating those learning experiences* (Brockett and Hiemstra, 1991; Merriam and Caffarella, 1991).

The process of how learners go about taking the primary responsibility for their own learning has fascinated educators of adults for the last two decades (Long, 1992; Merriam and Caffarella, 1991). From the numerous studies of this process, three very different descriptions of how adults go about the business of learning have emerged. The most popular and most often quoted scenario of how adults learn is described by Tough (1979) and Knowles (1975). Their descriptions imply that adults use a mostly linear, stepwise process (for example, identify their learning needs and decide which activities, methods, and techniques they will use). Their conception of the process of learning mirrors very closely how we depict the process of learning in formal settings.

A second scenario of the learning process is not so well planned or linear in nature; instead, there is an emphasis on opportunities that people find within their own environments or on chance occurrences (Berger, 1990; Candy, 1991; Danis and Tremblay, 1987; Spear and Mocker, 1984). What is stressed is that adults do not sit down and plan exactly what they want and where and when they are going to learn. Rather, the process is more haphazard in nature and is often a series of trial-and-error occurrences. This does not mean that there is no pattern to their learning, but the patterns vary from person to person and learning project to learning project. In essence, what emerges from this scenario "is a picture of the enormous complexity and unpredictability of a learning effort" (Candy, 1991, p. 172).

Recently, Cavaliere (1992) proposed a third scenario, as a result of her study of how the Wright brothers learned to fly. She identified five specific stages of their learning project: (1) inquiring (a need to solve a problem), (2) modeling (observing similar phenomena and developing a prototype model), (3) experimenting and practicing (continuous refinement and practice with the model), (4) theorizing and perfecting (perfection of their skills and the product), and (5) actualizing (receiving recognition for the product of their learning efforts). Within each of these five steps, four "repetitive cognitive processes (goal setting, focusing, persevering and reformulation) occurred . . . with a clearly identifiable breakpoint [between stages], preceded by frustration and confusion on the part of the Wright Brothers" (Cavaliere, 1992, p. 53). As with the second scenario, the importance of a set of specific opportunities and resources within the Wright brothers' own environment was critical to the success of their learning endeavor. This is the most sophisticated data-based model of how adults learn and is especially useful in that it describes not only the stages of the learning process but also the cognitive processes used throughout a major learning endeavor.

Learner Characteristics and Preferences. Definition and debate of the salient characteristics of adult learners constitute the second major contribution of the study of self-directed learning. The central assumption underlying this work on learner characteristics is that learning in adulthood means growth in self-direction and autonomy (Candy, 1991; Chene, 1983; Kasworm, 1983; Knowles, 1980). Recall that one of Knowles's four major tenets of andragogy is that "adults have a deep psychological need to be generally self-directing" (1980, p. 43). This learner characteristic of adults has become for many adult educators one of the major goals of their instructional processes: allowing and, in some cases, teaching adults how to take more responsibility and control in the learning process.

A central component of this conception of adults as self-directed learners is the notion of autonomy. Chene (1983), for example, has described three major elements that describe an autonomous learner: independence, the ability to make choices, and the capacity to articulate the norms and limits of a learning society. Candy (1991) adds to Chene's notion of the autonomous learner by characterizing autonomous people as those with a strong sense of personal values and beliefs. These values and beliefs give them a solid foundation for conceiving goals and plans, exercising free choice, using rationale reflection, having the will power to follow through, and exercising self-restraint and self-discipline (Candy, 1991, p. 125). The same overarching concepts of self-responsibility and control over actions in learning are also highlighted by Brockett and Hiemstra (1991) and Garrison (1992).

There have been challenges, stemming from the work on self-directed learning, to the assumption that the hallmark of the adult learner is autonomy and individual self-direction. For example, although Boucouvalas (1988) accepts that autonomy is an important characteristic of adult learners, she also argues that autonomy must be coupled with interdependence and interconnectedness as necessary attributes of adult learners. This same sentiment has been expressed by numerous scholars, writing primarily from the feminist tradition (Belenky, Clinchy, Goldberger, and Tarule, 1986; Caffarella, 1993; Hayes, 1989; Shrewsbury, 1987).

A second major challenge, primarily stemming from those authors who support the notion that self-direction and autonomy are key characteristics of adult learners, is that the choice of being self-directed and acting in an autonomous manner in a learning situation is not an all-or-nothing position. Even those adults who can or want to be self-directed in their learning may choose not to exhibit or pursue this characteristic at certain times (Brockett and Hiemstra, 1991; Candy, 1991; Pratt, 1988). Even Knowles (1975, 1980), in his earliest description of andragogy, qualified his notion that adults are naturally self-directing when he observed that people move toward self-directedness at differing rates and not necessarily in all dimensions of life, and that in some situations adults may need to be at least "temporarily dependent" in the learning situation. Four variables that appear to have the most influence on whether adult learners exhibit autonomous behavior in learning situations are their level of technical skills, their familiarity with subject matter, their sense of personal competence as learners, and the context of the learning event (Brockett and Hiemstra, 1991; Candy, 1991; Pratt, 1988).

Fostering Learner Initiative and Control in Formal Settings. This third contribution of self-direction to our understanding of learning has been widely discussed. For some adult educators, it is a major goal (Brockett and Hiemstra, 1991; Caffarella and Caffarella, 1986; Candy, 1991; Grow, 1991; Hammond and Collins, 1991; Hiemstra and Sisco, 1990; Kasworm, 1992; Knowles, 1975; Tough, 1979). Again, Tough (1979) and Knowles (1975) were among the first to urge that learner self-direction be incorporated into organized learning. Greater learner control means that learners are given the time and opportunity to think about what they want to learn (that is, what is meaningful or useful to them), how they want to go about learning (techniques, resources needed, location, and pacing), and which criteria will be used, and in what ways, to determine whether the learning experience was satisfactory and worthwhile. This learner control, according to Pratt (1988), comes in different forms, from learners wanting the instructor to primarily provide both the direction (what to learn) and the support (ways to go about learning), to learners being highly capable of providing their own direction and support. As noted in the previous subsection, the willingness and ability of the learner, the content to be learned, and the situational context influence the amount of self-direction and learner control that students are willing to take and instructors are willing to allow in formal settings.

A number of ideas have been advanced that describe how greater learner self-direction can be incorporated into formal instructional settings. Knowles (1975) developed a guide for learners and teachers about self-directed learning. The most useful part of this guide is a step-by-step outline for designing individual learning plans, including a description of the ways in which teachers and learners can work together to establish such plans. Knowles's basic format has been adopted by numerous others in their work with adult learners (Hiemstra and Sisco, 1990; Knowles, 1986; O'Donnell and Caffarella, 1990).

Hiemstra and Sisco (1990), Grow (1991), and Hammond and Collins

(1991) have posited specific models of instruction that foster greater self-direction by students. Hiemstra and Sisco, for example, outline a six-step individualization process that focuses primarily on the instructor's role. In this process, instructors become involved in the identification of learner resources prior to ever meeting with the students and continue with this facilitation role throughout the learning process by helping learners clarify education needs, choose appropriate learning activities, and identify useful evaluation strategies. In addition, the instructors also take on the more traditional instructional roles of content giver and monitor of activities. Grow's model, staged self-directed learning, like the Hiemstra and Sisco model, also outlines how instructors can help students to become more self-directed in their learning. Within each of the four stages of Grow's model, possible roles for teachers are offered that vary according to the learners' willingness and ability to be self-directed.

Hammond and Collins (1991), as described earlier, have taken a different tack for integrating self-directed learning into formal education programs. They have merged the idea of self-direction in learning with the notion of critical practice; that is, learner-centered instruction and critical analysis are key parts of the instructional process. They have outlined a nine-step procedure, which in some ways mirrors other program planning models (for example, Knowles, 1980; Sork and Caffarella, 1989), including such components as building a cooperative learning climate, analyzing the situation, diagnosing learner needs, and evaluating and validating learning. Hammond and Collins's proposal is different from these other planning models in the continuous integration of critical analysis and reflection into all but the "drafting learning agreement" step of the process.

Candy (1991) also offers useful insights into learner control of instruction and suggests ways in which to move from teacher control to learner control. He highlights the difficulties that teachers often have in making this transition, among them the major shift in the locus of control and how they have acted in the past as instructors. The task of serving as a facilitator of learning (that is, acting as a guide, coach, counselor, and/or evaluator) is quite different from that of telling students what they ought to know and how they ought to learn it. Candy also addresses the roles of learners and stresses that they may not always want or know how to take more control of their own learning and may actually resent having to participate in this kind of instructional activity. Fundamental changes in attitudes and beliefs of both teachers and learners about what constitutes formal instruction are needed for learner self-direction to become a major part of an institution's education program.

Self-Directed Learning: Impact and Promise

Knowledge about self-directed learning has had a significant impact on our understanding of learning in adulthood. As discussed in this chapter, we have a better picture of how adults learn, which key factors influence whether or not learners assume primary responsibility for their own learning, why the concept of autonomy appears to be a key descriptor of adult learners, and how adult educators can help learners take more control of their own learning within formal learning settings. However, caution needs to be exercised in using this knowledge base on self-directed learning to inform our thinking about learning in adulthood. For example, we should not idealize self-directed learning as the true mark of a mature adult learner. In addition, there are still numerous questions and debates about what constitutes self-directed learning and how this form of learning should be studied (Brockett and Hiemstra, 1991; Candy, 1991; Danis, 1992).

Yet, the study of self-directed learning continues to hold promise for assisting adult educators in their theory building and practice in the arena of adult learning (Caffarella, 1992; Garrison, 1992; Jarvis, 1990). What we know about self-directed learning might further inform our thinking, especially in the areas of information processing, adult cognitive development, and adult intelligence. There may be data within the completed descriptive studies of self-directed learning (for example, Cavaliere, 1992; Spear and Mocker, 1984; Tough, 1979) that could be used to answer a variety of questions about learning in adulthood. These data "might give us some insights into: the differences between novice and expert learners (Chi, Glaser, and Farr, 1988); how adults develop in their thinking over the life of a learning project, especially those projects of a long-term nature (Perry, 1981; Rybash, Hoyer, and Roodin, 1986); and what kinds of intelligence these adults exhibit (Gardner, 1983; Sternberg, 1988)" (Caffarella, 1992, p. 125). Garrison (1992) provides a good example of this type of work. He advocates a merging of the frameworks of self-directed learning and critical thinking, using the concepts of control and responsibility to offer a more integrative and explanatory view of adult learning.

In summary, what we know about self-directed learning, as reviewed in this chapter, is and will continue to be fundamental to how we as adult educators view learners, understand the learning process, act as instructors and facilitators, and serve as models of lifelong learners to those with whom we work and play. The ability to be self-directed in one's learning, that is, to be primarily responsible and in control of what, where, and how one learns, is critical to survival and prosperity in a world of continuous personal, community, and societal changes. The example of Brenda, a woman who had been diagnosed with breast cancer, whom I cited in a recent publication (Merriam and Caffarella, 1991) to illustrate the central characteristics of a self-directed learner, warrants mention here again. Little did I know that I would become like Brenda just shortly before the book was published. Like Brenda, I became, after much anguish and soul searching, highly self-directed in my learning so as to be an active member in the treatment and now the wellness teams. So, too, in communities and society in general, as with personal life events, there is a continuous need for people to be active and informed learners. If we are to cope with issues such as AIDS, hunger, homelessness, and social injustice, we must have the ability and willingness to be learners throughout our adult lives.

References

Belenky, M. F., Clinchy, B. M., Goldberger, N. R., and Tarule, J. M. *Women's Ways of Knowing: The Development of Self, Voice, and Mind.* New York: Basic Books, 1986.

Berger, N. "A Qualitative Study of the Process of Self-Directed Learning." Unpublished doctoral dissertation, Division of Educational Studies, Virginia Commonwealth University, 1990.

Boucouvalas, M. "An Analysis and Critique of the Concept of Self in Self-Directed Learning: Towards a More Robust Construct for Research and Practice." In M. Zukas (ed.), *Papers from the Transatlantic Dialogue.* Leeds, England: Standing Conference on University Teaching and Research in the Education of Adults, University of Leeds, 1988.

Brockett, R. G., and Hiemstra, R. *Self-Direction in Adult Learning: Perspectives on Theory, Research, and Practice.* New York: Routledge & Kegan Paul, 1991.

Brookfield, S. D. "Self-Directed Adult Learning: A Critical Paradigm." *Adult Education Quarterly,* 1984, *35,* 59–71.

Brookfield, S. D. *Understanding and Facilitating Adult Learning: A Comprehensive Analysis of Principles and Effective Practices.* San Francisco: Jossey-Bass, 1986.

Caffarella, R. S. "Research in Self-Directed Learning: Some Critical Observations." In H. B. Long and Associates, *Self-Directed Learning: Application and Research.* Stillwater: Research Center for Continuing Professional and Higher Education, University of Oklahoma, 1992.

Caffarella, R. S. *Psychosocial Development of Women: Linkages to Teaching and Leadership in Adult Education.* Columbus, Ohio: ERIC Clearinghouse on Adult, Career, and Vocational Education, 1993.

Caffarella, R. S., and Caffarella, E. P. "Self-Directedness and Learning Contracts in Adult Education." *Adult Education Quarterly,* 1986, *36,* 226–234.

Caffarella, R. S., and O'Donnell, J. M. "Self-Directed Adult Learning: A Critical Paradigm Revisited." *Adult Education Quarterly,* 1987, *37,* 199–211.

Caffarella, R. S., and O'Donnell, J. M. *Self-Directed Learning.* Nottingham, England: Department of Adult Education, University of Nottingham, 1989.

Caffarella, R. S., and O'Donnell, J. M. "Judging the Quality of Work-Related Self-Directed Learning." *Adult Education Quarterly,* 1991, *42,* 17–29.

Candy, P. C. *Self-Direction for Lifelong Learning: A Comprehensive Guide to Theory and Practice.* San Francisco: Jossey-Bass, 1991.

Cavaliere, L. A. "The Wright Brothers' Odyssey: Their Flight of Learning." In L. A. Cavaliere and A. Sgroi (eds.), *Learning for Personal Development.* New Directions for Adult and Continuing Education, no. 53. San Francisco: Jossey-Bass, 1992.

Chene, A. "The Concept of Autonomy: A Philosophical Discussion." *Adult Education Quarterly,* 1983, *34,* 38–47.

Chi, M.T.H., Glaser, R., and Farr, M. J. (eds.). *The Nature of Expertise.* Hillsdale, N.J.: Erlbaum, 1988.

Confessore, G. J., and Confessore, S. J. *Guideposts to Self-Directed Learning: Expert Commentary on Essential Concepts.* King of Prussia, Pa.: Organizational Design and Development, 1992.

Danis, C. "A Unifying Framework for Data-Based Research into Adult Self-Directed Learning." In H. B. Long and Associates, *Self-Directed Learning: Application and Research.* Stillwater: Research Center for Continuing Professional and Higher Education, University of Oklahoma, 1992.

Danis, C., and Tremblay, N. A. "Propositions Regarding Autodidactic Learning and Their Implications for Teaching." *Lifelong Learning: An Omnibus of Practice and Research,* 1987, *10* (7), 4–7.

Gardner, H. *Frames of Mind.* New York: Basic Books, 1983.

Garrison, D. R. "Critical Thinking and Self-Directed Learning in Adult Education: An Analysis of Responsibility and Control Issues." *Adult Education Quarterly,* 1992, *42,* 136–148.

Gerstner, L. S. "On the Theme and Variations of Self-Directed Learning: An Exploration of the Literature." Unpublished doctoral dissertation, Teachers College, Columbia University, 1987.

Gerstner, L. S. "What's in a Name? The Language of Self-Directed Learning." In H. B. Long and Associates, *Self-Directed Learning: Application and Research.* Stillwater: Research Center for Continuing Professional and Higher Education, University of Oklahoma, 1992.

Grow, G. O. "Teaching Learners to Be Self-Directed: A Stage Approach." *Adult Education Quarterly,* 1991, *41,* 125–149.

Hammond, M., and Collins, R. *Self-Directed Learning.* London: Kogan Page, 1991.

Hayes, E. R. "Insights from Women's Experiences for Teaching and Learning." In E. R. Hayes (ed.), *Effective Teaching Styles.* New Directions for Adult and Continuing Education, no. 43. San Francisco: Jossey-Bass, 1989.

Hiemstra, R. "Individualizing the Instructional Process: What We Have Learned from Two Decades of Research on Self-Direction in Learning." In H. B. Long and Associates, *Self-Directed Learning: Application and Research.* Stillwater: Research Center for Continuing Professional and Higher Education, University of Oklahoma, 1992.

Hiemstra, R., and Sisco, B. *Individualizing Instruction: Making Learning Personal, Empowering, and Successful.* San Francisco: Jossey-Bass, 1990.

Houle, C. O. *The Inquiring Mind.* Madison: University of Wisconsin Press, 1961.

Jarvis, P. "The Future of Self-Directed Learning Research." Paper presented at the annual meeting of the Commission of Professors of Adult Education, Salt Lake City, Utah, October 1990.

Kasworm, C. E. "Toward a Paradigm of Developmental Levels of Self-Directed Learning." Paper presented at the annual meeting of the American Educational Research Association, Montreal, Quebec, Canada, April 1983.

Kasworm, C. E. "Adult Learners in Academic Settings: Self-Directed Learning Within the Formal Learning Context." In H. B. Long and Associates, *Self-Directed Learning: Application and Research.* Stillwater: Research Center for Continuing Professional and Higher Education, University of Oklahoma, 1992.

Knowles, M. S. *Self-Directed Learning.* New York: Association Press, 1975.

Knowles, M. S. *The Modern Practice of Adult Education: From Pedagogy to Andragogy.* (2nd ed.) New York: Cambridge Books, 1980.

Knowles, M. S. *Using Learning Contracts: Practical Approaches to Individualizing and Structuring Learning.* San Francisco: Jossey-Bass, 1986.

Long, H. B. "Learning About Self-Directed Learning." In H. B. Long and Associates, *Self-Directed Learning: Application and Research.* Stillwater: Research Center for Continuing Professional and Higher Education, University of Oklahoma, 1992.

Long, H. B., and Associates. *Self-Directed Learning: Application and Research.* Stillwater: Research Center for Continuing Professional and Higher Education, University of Oklahoma, 1992.

Merriam, S. B., and Caffarella, R. S. *Learning in Adulthood: A Comprehensive Guide.* San Francisco: Jossey-Bass, 1991.

Mezirow, J. D. "A Critical Theory of Self-Directed Learning." In S. D. Brookfield (ed.), *Self-Directed Learning: From Theory to Practice.* New Directions for Adult and Continuing Education, no. 25. San Francisco: Jossey-Bass, 1985.

O'Donnell, J. M., and Caffarella, R. S. "Learning Contracts." In M. W. Galbraith (ed.), *Adult Learning Methods*. Malabar, Fla.: Krieger, 1990.

Perry, W. "Cognitive and Ethical Growth: The Making of Meaning." In A. W. Chickering and Associates, *The Modern American College: Responding to the New Realities of Diverse Students and a Changing Society*. San Francisco: Jossey-Bass, 1981.

Pratt, D. D. "Andragogy as a Relational Construct." *Adult Education Quarterly*, 1988, *38*, 160–181.

Rybash, J. M., Hoyer, W. J., and Roodin, P. A. *Adult Cognition and Aging*. Elmsford, N.Y.: Pergamon Press, 1986.

Shrewsbury, C. M. "What Is Feminist Pedagogy?" *Women's Studies Quarterly*, 1987, *15* (3), 6–14.

Sork, T. J., and Caffarella, R. S. "Planning Programs for Adults." In S. B. Merriam and P. M. Cunningham (eds.), *Handbook of Adult and Continuing Education*. San Francisco: Jossey-Bass, 1989.

Spear, G. E., and Mocker, D. W. "The Organizing Circumstance: Environmental Determinants in Self-Directed Learning." *Adult Education Quarterly*, 1984, *35*, 1–10.

Sternberg, R. J. *The Triarchic: A New Theory of Human Intelligence*. New York: Viking Press, 1988.

Tough, A. *Learning Without a Teacher*. Educational Research Series, no. 3. Toronto, Ontario, Canada: Ontario Institute for Studies in Education, 1967.

Tough, A. *The Adult's Learning Projects: A Fresh Approach to Theory and Practice in Adult Learning*. (2nd ed.) Toronto, Ontario, Canada: Ontario Institute for Studies in Education, 1979.

ROSEMARY S. CAFFARELLA is associate professor in the Division of Educational Leadership and Policy Studies, College of Education, University of Northern Colorado, Greeley.

Three adult learning theories or models that have not been adequately researched are described and analyzed in terms of their potential for increasing our knowledge of adult learning.

Three Underdeveloped Models for Adult Learning

Roger Hiemstra

As shown in other chapters of this volume, there have been several efforts to construct theories or models that explain how and why adults learn. Some have been more successful than others. A few have drawn considerable attention in the literature. This chapter presents three additional models that have not received as much attention and consequently have remained in the same forms as proposed by their originators. These models are discussed in terms of their origins, the original underlying assumptions or purposes, and the contributions made to our understanding of adult learning. I also describe a few instances where further research on them has been conducted. In addition, I speculate on why each has retained some "popularity" and consider their potential usefulness.

Chain of Response and Characteristics of Adults as Learners

K. Patricia Cross, although not trained for a career in or as a practitioner of adult education, made a significant impact on the field with several publications during the 1970s and early 1980s. Some of her initial work was with the Commission on Non-Traditional Study. She was involved with several publications that provided foundational support for various efforts in the United States to develop adult nontraditional study opportunities (Cross, 1971, 1976; Cross, Valley, and Associates, 1974; Gould and Cross, 1972).

Cross's most important work is *Adults as Learners: Increasing Participation and Facilitating Learning,* published in 1981. This book was designed to synthesize much of the information available regarding adult learning and served as a primary text for several years in many North American graduate courses related to adult learning. She popularized information about barriers to adult learning, studies of participation, and developmental stages. She also introduced two conceptual frameworks to describe various aspects of adult learning and to stimulate related research.

The first of these frameworks, the Chain of Response (COR) model, pertains to adult participation in learning: "[This is] the rough beginning of a conceptual framework designed to identify the relevant variables and hypothesize their interrelationships" (Cross, 1981, p. 124). Reynolds (1986) described how Cross delineated common elements of earlier participation models for the COR model: (1) Motivation to participate is the result of an individual's perception of both positive and negative forces. (2) Certain personality types are difficult to attract to education because of low self-esteem. (3) There is congruence between participation and anticipated learning outcomes. (4) Higher-order needs for achievement and self-actualization cannot be fulfilled until lower-order needs for security and safety are met. And (5) expectations of reward are important to motivation.

Arrows show one- or two-way relationships among seven elements of the model, including (1) self-evaluation, which is interrelated with (2) attitudes about education, (3) importance of making and meeting goals, which is affected by (4) life transactions and also interrelated with (5) opportunities and barriers, which in turn are affected by (6) information about the environment and impact on (7) participation, which in turn impacts on (3). Cross believed that this model should not be viewed as linear, although her two-dimensional depiction is visually linear. As Merriam and Caffarella (1991, p. 237) note, it is "also a reciprocal model in that participation in adult education . . . can affect how one feels about education . . . and oneself as a learner."

For the second of her conceptual frameworks, Characteristics of Adults as Learners (CAL), Cross (1981, p. 234) observed, "I offer the following model as a tentative framework to accommodate current knowledge about what we know about adults as learners, in the hope that it may suggest ideas for further research and for implementation." Her purpose was to describe differences between adults and children so that alternative teaching strategies could be developed.

The model's visual depiction shows two classes of variables: (1) *personal characteristics,* including physiological/aging and sociocultural/ life phases and psychological/developmental stages and (2) *situational characteristics,* including part-time learning versus full-time learning and voluntary learning versus compulsory learning. The personal characteristics are depicted as continuous in nature, with before and after arrows used to enhance this visual image. The situational variables are intended to show primarily dichotomous relationships. Cross included a second figure with three continua depicting each characteristic's continuous nature.

She also provided detailed information about the personal and situational characteristics, wove in information about available research, and included examples of how people might exhibit certain characteristics. She concluded by discussing implications in terms of current or needed research. Referring to her two conceptual frameworks and other research described in the book, she noted, "I hope and believe that many of the questions educators have about adult learning will be illuminated by the research reported in this book, but I hope even more strongly that readers will be helped to formulate new questions and to think in new ways about the future of the learning society" (Cross, 1981, p. 249).

In terms of contributions to our understanding of adult learning, one of Cross's goals was to synthesize the work of several adult education scholars. For example, she believed that some "of the assumptions of andragogy can be incorporated into [the] CAL construct" (Cross, 1981, p. 238). These included such notions as readiness and self-concept. The CAL framework also provided a means for thinking about the ever-changing adult in terms of developmental stages.

Many aspects of what is known about participation were included in the COR model. Other researchers have used such information in their own studies. For example, Beaudin (1982) reviewed literature on student retention and described the COR model as a means for understanding participation. Reynolds (1986) sought to refine the COR model and explain who participates in learning activities by examining measures of self-actualization and self-directed readiness among adult community college students. However, Cross (1981, p. 130) believed that the psychological aspects of her COR model were the most important: "If adult educators wish to understand why some adults fail to participate in learning opportunities, they need to begin at the beginning of the COR model—with an understanding of attitudes toward self and education."

Educators can use such models to stimulate various research projects. In essence, many interrelationships in the COR model are potential research topics. For example, we need to know more about how people formulate and use goals in relation to attitudes about education. Are there other personal or situational characteristics that need to be identified? Perhaps it will be possible for future researchers to create self-diagnostic procedures whereby learners can better understand the forces that Cross suggests impact on learning efforts.

Proficiency Theory of Adult Learning

Alan B. Knox, adult education professor at the University of Wisconsin, has long been interested in various aspects of adult learning. A 1958 doctoral graduate of Syracuse University, he has been writing about adults as learners for nearly forty years. His 1977 and 1986 books, for example, provided comprehensive information regarding both adult learning and teaching adults.

Knox (1979b) also developed the inaugural volume of the New Directions for Adult and Continuing Education series and served as the series editor-in-chief for several years. In the first volume, he dealt extensively with what he called practitioner proficiency: "It has become increasingly important that continuing education practitioners understand major areas of proficiency which contribute to their effectiveness, along with ways to acquire and use such proficiencies" (Knox, 1979a, p. 1). Knox believed that to be successful, continuing educators need to develop deliberate strategies for increasing personal proficiency.

He identified major areas of proficiency to be woven into strategies for helping adults learn, including understanding the field of continuing education, understanding adults as learners, having a positive attitude toward lifelong learning, and obtaining effective interpersonal relationship skills. He also outlined specific areas of proficiency for administrators, teachers, counselors, and policymakers.

In one of his first published discussions of ideas about proficiency as part of a theory, Knox (1980, p. 382) noted that "proficiency theory provides a parsimonious explanation of the teaching-learning transaction for adults in all its variety, and contains generalizations regarding human learning . . . as well as generalizations that are especially important for adults with various characteristics, such as learning ability, age, and experience." He defined proficiency as "the capability to perform satisfactorily if given the opportunity" (p. 378), with performance referring to some combination of attitude, knowledge, and skill.

He began to talk about the need for teachers and learners to understand discrepancies that might exist between current and desired proficiencies. He believed that the use of needs assessment and evaluation activities to examine proficiencies was necessary: "An understanding of discrepancies between current and desired proficiencies helps to explain motives of adult learners and enables those who help adults learn to do so responsively and effectively" (Knox, 1986, p. 16).

Knox believes that proficiency-oriented learning has potential for helping adults achieve at the highest possible level. In comparing proficiency ideas with competence-based approaches, he noted that "whereas competency-based preparatory education emphasizes the achievement of minimal standards of performance in educational tasks, proficiency-oriented continuing education emphasizes achievement of optimal standards of proficiency related to adult life roles" (Knox, 1986, p. 16). This idea of promoting excellence or optimal learning remains an attractive feature of his theory.

In terms of contributions to our understanding of adult learning, Merriam and Caffarella (1991, p. 255) suggest that proficiency theory contains several interactive components: "the general [societal] environment, past and current [personal] characteristics, performance, aspiration, self, discrepancies, specific [learning] environments, learning activity, and the teacher's role." Knox (1985, p. 252) indicated how the theory might be useful: "[The theory] suggests fundamental relationships among essential aspects of adult learning and teaching which constitute an interrelated set of guidelines for helping adults learn, with an emphasis on motivation."

Thus, instructors can use techniques or instruments designed to gain knowledge about any of the components. For example, suggestions for analyzing aspects of a learning environment are available (Hiemstra, 1991). The practices of engaging learners in conversations, promoting self-reflection, and asking learners to develop learning plans that show how proficiencies will be increased are other possible techniques.

In my courses, I ask learners to carry out self-assessments on various knowledge areas and personal characteristics. I also ask learners to complete learning contracts and provide them with proficiency models against which they can compare their own needs and aspirations. These kinds of planning activities typically provide learners with basic information about current proficiencies and serve to guide their future learning efforts. Future research on the use of such techniques will refine our knowledge about Knox's model and proficiency areas.

Theory of Margin

Howard Y. McClusky, a professor of educational psychology and adult education at the University of Michigan from 1924 until his death in 1982, looked at adult learning through the eyes of a person trained in experimental psychology. He was long concerned with finding ways to help adults maintain a productive posture in meeting the requirements of living. Early in his career he worked primarily with young adults. Then, as he aged, his concerns shifted to adults at later ages (Hiemstra, 1981). He focused primarily on adults in retirement during his last fifteen years.

He introduced the theory of margin thirty years ago (McClusky, 1963). He felt that the theory was relevant for understanding adults' physical and mental well-being, especially during their later years when various demands or pressures might increase. McClusky believed that adulthood involved continuous growth, change, and integration, in which constant effort must be made to wisely use the energy available for meeting the normal responsibilities of living. However, because people have less than perfect control over many aspects of life, they must always be prepared to meet unexpected crises or problems.

Margin was conceived as a formula expressing a ratio or relationship between "load" (of living) and "power" (to carry the load). According to McClusky (1970, p. 27), load is "the self and social demands required by a person to maintain a minimal level of autonomy. . . . [Power is] the resources, i.e. abilities, possessions, position, allies, etc., which a person can command in coping with *load*." In this formula for margin (M), he placed designations of load (L) in the numerator and designations of power (P) in the denominator (M = L/P).

He further divided load into two groups of interacting elements, one external and the other internal. The external load consists of tasks involved in normal life requirements (such as family, work, and community responsibilities). Internal load consists of life expectancies developed by people (such as aspirations, desires, and future expectations). Power consists of a combination of such external resources and capacity as family support, social abilities, and economic abilities. It also includes various internally acquired or accumulated skills and experiences contributing to effective performance, such as resilience, coping skills, and personality.

Thus, a person's performance is a function of various load dimensions and values, as well as a capacity to carry the load. Margin can be increased by reducing load or increasing power. McClusky (1963) suggested that surplus power is always needed to provide enough margin or cushion to meet various load requirements and life emergencies.

In terms of contributions to our understanding of adult learning, for most adults a grasp of what McClusky developed is an epiphany in terms of their own life circumstances. The balancing of demands on life with goals or interests requires the maintenance of some sort of margin. Thus, instructors should help learners discover aspects of the theory of margin.

The theory also can serve as a guide to explain at least some of the events that happen throughout life. McClusky (1963) believed that the value of the theory was its usefulness in describing varying amounts of margin that could be involved in adult adjustment. Such value is directly observable when applying the theory to learning activities by adults in their later years, a period in which radical changes in the load-power ratio may take place due to declining financial resources, death of a spouse, and so forth. As McClusky (1970, p. 146) observed, "In the light of our theory therefore, a necessary condition for learning is access to and/or the activation of a Margin of Power that may be available for application to the processes which the learning situation requires."

Thus, a crucial element for meeting learning or other life demands is the ratio between load and power: "Whatever the load and whatever the power (up to a practical level), the crucial element is the surplus or margin of power in excess of load. It is this margin that confers autonomy on the individual, gives him an opportunity to examine a range of options, and enables him to reinvest his psychological capital in growth and development" (McClusky, n.d., p. 330). Frequently, learning during the adult years provides surplus power and becomes a major force in achieving various goals.

THREE UNDERDEVELOPED MODELS   43

There are various ways in which an instructor can unknowingly generate excess load for a learner. If an instructor assumes a traditional, authoritarian attitude, learners may feel frustrated or sense that their opinions are being ignored. An instructor may seem disorganized or have distracting mannerisms that serve to discourage the learner. If inappropriate assignments are given or any evaluation guidelines are unclear, some adults will have difficulties. Thus, if an instructor pays little attention to the task of creating an effective learning environment, some adults will experience increased loads due to distracting physical, social, or psychological features (Hiemstra and Sisco, 1990).

Margin theory also can be used as a research framework. For example, Baum (1978) studied widowhood and used margin theory as a conceptual framework. Gessner (1979) used margin as a theoretical framework for studying nurses' participation in continuing education. Gleit (1976) used the theory to look at potential restrictions to participation in continuing education. Garrison (1986), James (1986), Mikolaj (1983), and Stevenson (1982) have attempted to measure aspects of power and load.

Finally, margin theory can be used as a basis for practical applications. Main (1979) conceptualized a teaching and learning model based on power and load notions. Hiemstra (1981) proposed a framework for planning education programs based on load and power imbalances, including examples for how the framework can be used.

Why Have These Theories Remained Popular?

Although the theories or models described in this chapter have not been fully developed, each has retained some popularity and utility as measured in terms of citations in the literature or use as a basis for research. One reason for their staying power is the originators' charisma and reputations for prolific writing. McClusky was an enormously popular and admired teacher, leader, and author. He was highly respected and held in high esteem, and many people simply believed what he said about adults and learning. However, his theory does not specifically address the actual function and features of learning, so empirical testing has been difficult.

Knox, too, has charisma that attracts much respect. His visibility as a national leader, editor, and author has added "weight" to his conceptualizations. Unfortunately, as Merriam and Caffarella (1991, pp. 255–256) note, "Knox's theory is not well known by adult educators, perhaps because its publication has been in sources outside the field of adult education. . . . Its emphasis on performance . . . [limits] its application to learning . . . [and how] one tracks the interaction of ten components . . . to arrive at an explanation of how adults learn is far from clear."

Cross rapidly had a large impact on adult education with her many publications over a relatively short period. The popularity of her 1981 book also helped to lend credence to the conceptual work that she presented. Unfortunately, the variables that she has described seem too broadly defined and await refinement through future research.

Overall, there is considerable utility in the models and theories of these three authors. Adult educators can see practical applications in what they have proposed. For example, students can be helped to use their ideas in promoting personal change. Some people, when they understand what Cross, Knox, or McClusky have described, can immediately begin applying the concepts to their own situations. Thus, there is value in the contributions of these models even though they are not fully developed.

What Is Their Potential?

As theoretical models or frameworks, each proposal presented in this chapter has potential value. Each attempts to organize existing knowledge about adult involvement with learning into a visible or usable framework. As such, each provides a foundation for further testing and refinement.

For example, a better understanding of the interrelationship among various participation factors is possible through more work with the COR model. There is much more about proficiencies that needs to be understood, and Knox's proficiency theory is a good starting point. Although there have been several attempts to research aspects of margin theory, continued work can only serve to enhance at least part of McClusky's legacy.

As Brookfield (1992) notes, there are four criteria that must be met for a theory to be taken seriously: (1) the distinction, separateness, and discreteness of whatever phenomenon is being described, (2) the extent to which the phenomenon is grounded in observable and documented evidence, (3) the comprehensiveness of all aspects of the phenomenon, and (4) the extent to which the phenomenon can be examined for accuracy and validity by other researchers. Future researchers and practitioners can examine all four frameworks or theories discussed here in light of these criteria. It is my hope that this publication will stimulate such future study and enhance the viability and usefulness of these models as guides to our work with adult learners.

References

Baum, J. "An Exploration of Widowhood: Implications for Adult Educators." Paper presented at the 19th annual meeting of the Adult Education Research Conference, San Antonio, Texas, May 1978.

Beaudin, B. *Retaining Adult Students. Overview.* ERIC Fact Sheet No. 12. Columbus, Ohio: ERIC Clearinghouse on Adult, Career, and Vocational Education, 1982. (ED 237 800)

Brookfield, S. D. "Developing Criteria for Formal Theory Building in Adult Education." *Adult Education Quarterly*, 1992, 42, 79–93.

Cross, K. P. *Beyond the Open Door: New Students to Higher Education.* San Francisco: Jossey-Bass, 1971.

Cross, K. P. *Accent on Learning: Improving Instruction and Reshaping the Curriculum.* San Francisco: Jossey-Bass, 1976.

Cross, K. P. *Adults as Learners: Increasing Participation and Facilitating Learning.* San Francisco: Jossey-Bass, 1981.

Cross, K. P., Valley, J. R., and Associates. *Planning Non-Traditional Programs.* San Francisco: Jossey-Bass, 1974.

Garrison, D. R. "An Analysis and Reformulation of McClusky's Concept of Margin for Predicting Adult Dropout." Paper presented at the 27th annual meeting of the Adult Education Research Conference, Syracuse, New York, May 1986.

Gessner, B. A. "Margin and Its Relationship to Nurses' Participation in Continuing Professional Education." Unpublished doctoral dissertation, Department of Continuing and Vocational Education, University of Wisconsin, Madison, 1979.

Gleit, C. J. "Effects of Family Composition on the North Carolina Nursing Force and Their Participation in Continuing Education Programs." Unpublished doctoral dissertation, Department of Adult and Community College Education, North Carolina State University, 1976.

Gould, S. B., and Cross, K. P. (eds.). *Exploration in Non-Traditional Study.* San Francisco: Jossey-Bass, 1972.

Hiemstra, R. "The Contributions of Howard Yale McClusky to an Evolving Discipline of Educational Gerontology." *Educational Gerontology*, 1981, 6, 209–226.

Hiemstra, R. (ed.). *Creating Environments for Effective Adult Learning.* New Directions for Adult and Continuing Education, no. 50. San Francisco: Jossey-Bass, 1991.

Hiemstra, R., and Sisco, B. *Individualizing Instruction: Making Learning Personal, Empowering, and Successful.* San Francisco: Jossey-Bass, 1990.

James, J. M. "Instructor-Generated Load: An Inquiry Based on McClusky's Concepts of Margin." Unpublished doctoral dissertation, Department of Educational Administration and Adult Education, University of Wyoming, 1986.

Knox, A. B. *Adult Development and Learning: A Handbook on Individual Growth and Competence in the Adult Years.* San Francisco: Jossey-Bass, 1977.

Knox, A. B. "Overview: An Introduction to the Field." In A. B. Knox (ed.), *Enhancing Proficiencies of Continuing Educators.* New Directions for Adult and Continuing Education, no. 1. San Francisco: Jossey-Bass, 1979a.

Knox, A. B. (ed.). *Enhancing Proficiencies of Continuing Educators.* New Directions for Adult and Continuing Education, no. 1. San Francisco: Jossey-Bass, 1979b.

Knox, A. B. "Proficiency Theory of Adult Learning." *Contemporary Educational Psychology*, 1980, 5, 378–404.

Knox, A. B. "Adult Learning and Proficiency." In D. Kleiber and M. Maehr (eds.), *Advances in Motivation and Achievement.* Vol. 4: *Motivation in Adulthood.* Greenwood, Conn.: JAI Press, 1985.

Knox, A. B. *Helping Adults Learn: A Guide to Planning, Implementing, and Conducting Programs.* San Francisco: Jossey-Bass, 1986.

McClusky, H. Y. "Education for Aging: The Scope of the Field and Perspectives for the Future." In S. M. Grabowski and W. D. Mason (eds.), *Learning for Aging.* Washington, D.C.: Adult Education Association of the U.S.A., n.d.

McClusky, H. Y. "The Course of the Adult Life Span." In W. C. Hallenbeck (ed.), *Psychology of Adults.* Chicago: Adult Education Association of the U.S.A., 1963.

McClusky, H. Y. "An Approach to a Differential Psychology of the Adult Potential." In S. M. Grabowski (ed.), *Adult Learning and Instruction.* Syracuse, N.Y.: ERIC Clearinghouse on Adult Education, 1970. (ED 045 867)

Main, K. "The Power-Load-Margin Formula of Howard Y. McClusky as the Basis for a Model of Teaching." *Adult Education,* 1979, *30,* 19–33.

Merriam, S. B., and Caffarella, R. S. *Learning in Adulthood: A Comprehensive Guide.* San Francisco: Jossey-Bass, 1991.

Mikolaj, E. "The Intrapersonal Role Conflicts of Adult Women Undergraduate Students." Paper presented at the 24th annual meeting of the Adult Education Research Conference, Raleigh, North Carolina, May 1983.

Reynolds, M. M. "The Self-Direction and Motivational Orientations of Adult Part-Time Students at a Community College." Unpublished doctoral dissertation, Department of Adult Education, Syracuse University, 1986.

Stevenson, J. "Construction of a Scale to Measure Load, Power, and Margin in Life." *Nursing Research,* 1982, *31* (4), 222–225.

ROGER HIEMSTRA is professor and chair of adult education at Syracuse University, Syracuse, New York.

This chapter explores the work in transformational learning of Mezirow, Freire, and Daloz to identify the underlying humanistic assumptions of this type of learning and to assess its contribution to the field.

Transformational Learning

M. Carolyn Clark

Definitions are always a good place to begin, and in the case of *transformational learning* a clear definition seems to be implicit in the term itself: Transformation is about change, so transformational learning must be related to learning that produces change. But does not all learning result in change of some kind, whether of attitudes, skills, knowledge, or beliefs? What is different about the changes that transformational learning generates?

The immediate answer is that transformational learning produces more far-reaching changes in the learners than does learning in general, and that these changes have a significant impact on the learner's subsequent experiences. In short, transformational learning *shapes* people; they are different afterward, in ways both they and others can recognize. The process can be gradual or sudden, and it can occur in a structured education environment or in the classroom of ordinary life. Transformational learning is, in short, a normal part of our lives and intimately connected to the developmental process.

Let us consider our own lives. What experiences stand out in our memories that have shaped who we are? All of us can cite some of those predictable events that accompany changes in social roles: leaving home and establishing ourselves as autonomous adults, commiting ourselves to an intimate relationship, developing competence in a career, raising children, assuming responsibility for aging parents, retiring from a job. Then there are the unpredictable events that often occur without warning and that can be sources of pain or joy: the death of a loved one, the loss of a job, winning a national award, or coming into a large inheritance. In all cases, we can look back on these or similar marker experiences and identify the effects that they have had on our development, on who we are as human

New Directions for Adult and Continuing Education, no. 57, Spring 1993 © Jossey-Bass Publishers

beings. They have changed us. Before the experience we were one sort of person, but after we were another.

Transformations, whether dramatic or developmental, involve change. It is when we ask *how* those changes occurred that we begin exploring the territory of transformational learning. The goal of this chapter is to provide an overall sense of what that territory contains and the promise it holds for the understanding of other kinds of learning in adulthood.

Nature of Transformational Learning

The transformation process has been extensively studied by psychologists and by developmental theorists, but it is only within the past twenty years or so that it has become a subject of interest in adult education and thus conceptualized as a learning process. There are three strands to this area of study in our field: Jack Mezirow's theory of perspective transformation, the critical pedagogy of Paulo Freire, and the work of Laurent Daloz on the developmental character of formal education in adulthood. While related in significant ways conceptually, each has a different approach to the transformational learning process.

Mezirow's interests are theoretical. His primary purpose is to develop a comprehensive theory of adult learning that has as its centerpiece the structuring of meaning from experience. Mezirow argues that all human beings function within meaning systems, complex and dynamic structures of beliefs, theories, and psychocultural assumptions. These meaning systems function as a lens or filter through which personal experience is mediated and by which it is interpreted. While these structures organize our experience and make it coherent, they also distort perception to some degree by establishing what Mezirow (1990b, p. 2) calls "habits of expectation" that limit perception. Changes in meaning structures can occur incrementally or more suddenly, as is the case in perspective transformation. Central to that change process is critical reflection, where the underlying assumptions of the meaning perspective are identified, critically assessed, and reformulated to permit the development of a more inclusive and permeable meaning perspective. Mezirow's theory of learning is closely related to adult developmental theory, and, in fact, he understands the process of perspective transformation as "the central process of adult development" (Mezirow, 1991, p. 155).

While Mezirow's concept of transformational learning is directed toward personal development, Freire's idea of transformational learning has the ultimate goal of social change. Initially formulated in the context of literacy education for the poor of Brazil, his ideas have currency in any setting in which power is inequitably distributed. Freire seeks to liberate adults through a dialogic, problem-posing pedagogical style that challenges students to become aware of the oppressive social structures in their world, to understand how those structures have influenced their own thought, and to recognize their own power to change their world (Freire, 1973). This process, which he calls "conscientization," is achieved through a combination of action and reflection, or praxis. This style of education is collaborative rather than passive, a movement away from the traditional model, which Freire calls "banking education," and toward a model that supports the freedom and autonomy of learners (Freire, 1970). Freire acknowledges the political nature of his view of education, but he argues that education is never politically neutral since it either domesticates students by giving them the values of the dominant group or it liberates them by enabling them to reflect on their world and act to change it. Fundamental is his vision of a just society where all people can live freely and with dignity. He understands transformational learning as the means to realize this vision.

A third conceptualization of transformational learning is offered by Daloz. Unlike Mezirow or Freire, Daloz deals with transformation within the particular setting of formal education. His research (Daloz, 1986) focuses on adult students in nontraditional baccalaureate programs, but he believes that it is applicable to all adult students. He wants to know what impact education has on adult learners. Developmental theorists have shown that education stimulates personal development, but Daloz focuses on how this change is effected. His answer is that development is facilitated by a relationship of care between teachers and their students. He argues that growth is a risky and frightening business, much like a journey into the unknown. Students are challenged to let go of old conceptualizations of self and their world and to embrace new understandings; the presence of a knowledgeable and caring teacher or mentor makes such a journey into the unknown less frightening. Mentors facilitate this growth process by providing support, challenge, and vision. Daloz's goal is to challenge teachers to think about their teaching not so much in terms of developing competencies but rather in terms of fostering personal development.

Mezirow, Freire, and Daloz are all concerned with transformational learning, but, as we have seen, in very different ways. However, there are elements common to the work of all three, and these form definitional boundaries for our understanding of transformational learning. Broadly, these elements involve philosophical assumptions about the nature of human beings, beliefs about knowledge, and ideas about the relationship between the individual and society. Because Mezirow has developed the most extensive theoretical conceptualization of transformational learning, I use his work as the centerpoint of this discussion and relate the positions of Freire and Daloz to his ideas.

What Does It Mean to Be Human? Transformational learning rests on a humanistic understanding of the person. At the center of Mezirow's theory of perspective transformation is the concept of the "rational, autonomous, responsible adult" (Mezirow, 1985, p. 27). This view assumes that adults have the potential for a high level of freedom of thought and action. There is also a pervasive theme of control. While there are "libidinal, institutional, or environmental forces which limit our options and rational control over our lives" (Mezirow, 1981, p. 5), the goal of transformational learning is to gain "a crucial sense of agency over ourselves and our lives" (1981, p. 20), what Mezirow (1990a, p. 375) later described as "the way we control our experiences rather than be controlled by them."

A similar conception of the person is central to Freire's work as well. His whole method of teaching assumes that human beings are free to reflect on their situation and to take action to change it. In his writings he frequently contrasts human beings with animals, making the point that we alone can reflect on our relationship to the world and act on it. Animals exist *in* the world, but human beings exist in relationship *with* the world by our capacity for praxis, the reciprocal linkage of reflection and action. This is a fundamental humanist belief.

Daloz likewise shares this humanistic understanding of the person. He is committed to a belief in development as normative, what Carl Rogers (1979, p. 99) called the "actualizing tendency": "We can say that there is in every organism, at whatever level, an underlying flow of movement towards constructive fulfillment of its inherent possibilities. In [human beings], too, there is a natural tendency toward a more complex and complete development." For Daloz, as for Mezirow, the freedom of adults to act is directed toward their own growth and development. Daloz simply addresses the implications for educators as they foster that developmental process.

How Do We Know That Something Is True? Mezirow's theory of knowing is interpretive or constructivist. In this view, reality is less an objective fact and more a subjective construction by individuals and societies. People create knowledge. Mezirow's approach has been shaped in particular by Habermas's theory of communicative interests, a comprehensive theory of knowledge that is rooted in critical social theory. His particular concern is with the distinction that Habermas draws between two types of knowledge: instrumental knowledge, which is concerned broadly with problem solving, and communicative knowledge, which seeks to understand the meaning of events or concepts. Knowledge, therefore, is not a unified objective reality but is, instead, a complex construction that we create to serve different purposes.

Mezirow (1991, p. xiv) has identified several constructivist assumptions that undergird his theory: "Meaning exists within ourselves rather than in external forms such as books and . . . the personal meanings that we attribute to our experience are acquired and validated through human interaction and communication. . . . Since information, ideas, and contexts change, our present interpretations of reality are always subject to revision or replacement." The provisional character of knowledge is congruent with the dynamic process of learning that Mezirow describes in his theory.

For Mezirow, critical reflection, a highly rational process whereby the underlying premises of ideas are assessed and critiqued, is central to the process of knowing. To know whether our conclusions are true, however, we must validate them through rational discourse. Since all of our own interpretations are never without bias, only consensual validation can provide "our greatest assurance of objectivity" (Mezirow, 1990b, p. 10) about the outcome. Drawing on Habermas, Mezirow (1985, 1991) outlines a series of conditions for rational or ideal discourse that includes such elements as full information, the ability to objectively evaluate arguments, and freedom from self-deception or coercion. These define ideal conditions, however, and Mezirow (1989, p. 171) acknowledges that they are largely unattainable but that they serve as "a standard against which to assess educational and social practice." While Mezirow never clearly explains how rational discourse functions under less-than-ideal conditions, it is clear that, in his view, cogency of argument is the final arbiter on the validity of constructed knowledge. Rationality determines what is reliably known.

Freire's ideas are very much in accord with this view. He speaks of human beings as creators of knowledge in almost theological terms: "To exist, humanly, is to *name* the world, to change it. . . . [We] are not built in silence, but in word, in work, in action-reflection" (Freire, 1970, p. 76). The naming of the world is the means whereby adults find voice and begin their empowerment. The work of constructing truth is both a personal and a collective responsibility, and Freire equates it with the creation of culture. "We began with the conviction that the role of [humankind] was not only to be in the world, but to engage in relations with the world—that through acts of creation and recreation, [we] make cultural reality and thereby add to the natural world. . . . We were certain that [humankind's] relation to reality . . . results in knowledge" (Freire, 1973, p. 43).

Daloz likewise believes in the construction of knowledge, but for him the process is personal. "As human beings, we are active participants in the process of making meaning, of constructing ways of knowing the world that help it cohere in a way that makes sense for us" (Daloz, 1990, p. 8). Adults evolve new ways of constructing meaning as they develop, and he defines growth in those terms. He is probably closest to Mezirow here, except that he argues for a holistic rather than a highly rational process of change.

What Is the Relationship Between the Individual and Society? The final element common across the work in transformational learning relates to implicit social theory. What is the relationship between the individual and the social? What is the governing vision of society?

Most of the critical attention that Mezirow has received is in this area: overwhelmingly, the criticism has been that he has misappropriated a critical social theory for individualistic ends. Critics point to the gap between his focus on an internal process of individuals and the critical social theory of Habermas, which Mezirow uses to explain central elements of that process. Mezirow does evidence an underlying social theory, but it is not the radical theory articulated by Habermas. With Collard and Law (1989), I characterize Mezirow's social theory as more liberal democratic in nature, which is congruent with his conceptualization of human beings. For him, society is made up of autonomous, responsible individuals who, having chosen to change their meaning perspectives, can in turn act to change their world. "We must begin with individual perspective transformations before social transformations can succeed" (Mezirow, 1990a, p. 363). Change is incremental and reformist in this model, not revolutionary. Again, it is the individual who stands at the center of Mezirow's concept of society, and power is understood not in terms of structural relationships but rather in terms of human agency. It is a thoroughly liberal democratic view.

Freire appears to have a more radical view, yet he argues passionately for democracy as well. He views his type of education as a basis for the development of true democracy. "One subverts democracy . . . by making it irrational. . . . One defends democracy by leading it to the state Mannheim calls 'militant democracy'—a democracy which does not fear the people, which suppresses privilege, which can plan without becoming rigid, which defends itself without hate, which is nourished by a critical spirit rather than irrationality" (Freire, 1973, p. 58). It is, in fact, a radical democracy that Freire is trying to build.

Daloz approaches the question of the relationship between the individual and society in a less political fashion, but he too is guided by a fundamentally democratic vision. In arguing for personal growth and development as the goal of education, he places a premium on the higher stages of development, where there is a shift away from a separate and autonomous self and toward an acknowledgment of the interconnectedness of all things. That shift produces a sense of responsibility to a wider reality. In a recent address to continuing educators, Daloz (1990, p. 9) assessed the trends of the current age and concluded that it is essential that we join "our daughters and sons and with their sons and daughters down through the generations, in the work of tending the growth of a more adequate, just, and compassionate world." With Mezirow and Freire, he believes that we are responsible for the society in which we live.

What, then, are the common elements of transformational learning as evidenced in Mezirow, Freire, and Daloz? All share a humanistic vision of the person, believing that human beings are capable of change and free to act on the world. They understand knowledge as a construction that human beings make rather than an objective truth that they discover. And, finally, they presume a democratic vision of society in which individuals are responsible for their collective futures. These elements describe the common core beliefs that underlie these various strands of transformational learning.

How Is Our Understanding of Learning Transformed?

What contribution does this specific type of learning make to our understanding of adult learning in general? Does it illuminate more than its own corner of the learning process? The answer is a multifaceted yes.

On the level of definition, transformational learning adds a new dimension to adult learning. In their overview of adult learning theory, Merriam and Caffarella (1991) divide the landscape into three areas of focus: characteristics of adult learners, the life situations of adults, and changes in consciousness within the learner. It is the work of Mezirow and Freire that created this third category. Further, an understanding of learning as a change in consciousness carries theory to a new level. In theories of learning focused on either the life situations or adult characteristics of learners, we are dealing with *descriptions* of learners, their situations, or both, but the actual *process* of learning is not addressed. We see this process dealt with directly in transformational learning, in theoretical terms by Mezirow and in practical terms by Freire and Daloz.

Transformational learning also makes a contribution to our understanding of learning by construing learning in terms of meaning formation. Mezirow, Freire, and Daloz situate learning directly in the interpretation of experience: "No need is more fundamentally human than our need to understand the meaning of our experience" (Mezirow, 1990b, p. 11). The whole concept of learning is expanded here, to include all the ways in which adults revise their understanding of things as they engage life day by day. Learning becomes more inclusive, and more pervasive. If learning is the restructuring of meaning as adults engage life experience, then learning can be conceptualized as the vehicle of adult development. This is a considerable expansion of our understanding of the role of learning in adulthood.

Transformational learning also makes our understanding of learning more complex. No longer is it enough to speak of learning as behavioral change. The changes in consciousness evident in transformational learning cannot be understood in behavioral terms; we are thus challenged to attend to multiple psychosocial factors. Mezirow's theory certainly suggests greater complexity, but the pedagogies of Freire and Daloz also point to critical elements that must be given more consideration in the learning process. Reflection, for example, is central to these changes as it is to all learning, but its importance is highlighted in the transformational process since the focus is on a change in consciousness. In transformational learning, reflection is in some ways more visible and accessible, offering us an opportunity to learn more about the reflection process. Freire's concept of praxis, the inherent linkage of reflection and action, is an example of how our understanding of the reflective process is expanded. Further, the role of dialogue or discourse in the transformational learning process is stressed by all three. Discourse is reflection made public, which further contributes to our understanding of it.

Overall, we can say that transformational learning adds a new dimension to our conceptualization of learning in adulthood. By construing learning as meaning making that results in a change of consciousness, we can examine the process of learning from a different perspective. The result is a more complex understanding of the learning process.

Transformational Learning in Practice

The final question concerns the effect that transformational learning has had on practice. Where do we see examples of this kind of learning, apart from our own personal experiences of change?

The focus on change in consciousness is manifested in many ways and reflects the influence of Mezirow and Freire in particular. Probably the most dramatic example of transformational learning in practice is found in community-based adult education, particularly in organizations of popular education. Influenced by Freire and other philosophies of social change, popular education is populist in character and seeks "the development of a capacity to transform reality, and the strengthening of the organizational structure to challenge existing power arrangements" (Hamilton and Cunningham, 1989, p. 445). Popular education programs exist throughout the country, but the most prominent is the Highlander Research and Education Center in Tennessee. Founded by Myles Horton in 1932, it worked, first, with labor and civil rights movements and now is concerned with various groups of oppressed people, always with the goal of "educating for a revolution that would basically alter economic and political power relationships to the advantage of the poor and powerless" (Adams and Horton, 1975, p. 179). Freire has conducted workshops at Highlander several times, and the congruence between his ideas and the Highlander philosophy is clear.

Other examples of transformational learning in practice can be found in mainstream adult education. Take, for example, the current interest in critical thinking, perhaps best articulated by Brookfield (1991). Short courses and workshops to develop these skills are common in adult and continuing education programs around the country, as well as in corporate training sessions. Critical thinking draws liberally from Mezirow's theory of transformational learning. These ideas also are part of the foundation of the National Issues Forum (NIF), an organization of discussion groups committed to the development of an informed and responsible citizenry. NIF certainly demonstrates the democratic goals of transformational learning as well. It is noteworthy that this program has also been adapted for low-literate adults for use in adult basic education programs (see, for example, Hurley, 1991), where it has been successful.

There is also greater attention given to the transformative dimension of teaching. Mezirow and Associates (1990) discuss several ways that transformative learning can be facilitated to include such things as journaling, analyzing metaphors, doing life histories, and using literature to stimulate critical consciousness. They argue that transformational learning fits well with the general goals of adult education, which correlates with the view that adult development should be "the unifying idea" of higher education (Chickering, 1981, p. 2). Daloz has developed this idea further in his analysis of how development is fostered by the teacher-student relationship. The nontraditional college program that Daloz described, highly individualized in its curriculum, has become more and more popular with adult students. Halterman (1983) lists nontraditional programs in virtually every state in an effort to make these programs known and accessible to many adults who cannot attend traditional programs.

The presence of transformational learning in these diverse arenas attests to its important contribution to practice. While not a major thread in adult education offerings, it is nonetheless having a significant impact.

Conclusion

Transformational learning provides the field of adult education with new insights into the learning process. The different conceptualizations of this type of learning advanced by Mezirow, Freire, and Daloz all posit learning as a change in consciousness. Further, they share three humanistic assumptions: a view of human beings as free and responsible, an understanding of knowledge as a personal and social construction, and a belief in a liberal democratic vision of society. Transformational learning has widened our understanding of learning in adulthood by construing it in terms of meaning formation and highlighting the role of reflection. Altogether, it is reasonable to suggest that transformational learning has changed the landscape of adult learning and that it is having a discernible impact on practice.

References

Adams, F., and Horton, M. *Unearthing Seeds of Fire: The Idea of Highlander.* Winston-Salem, N.C.: Blair, 1975.

Brookfield, S. D. *Developing Critical Thinkers: Challenging Adults to Explore Alternative Ways of Thinking and Acting.* San Francisco: Jossey-Bass, 1991.

Chickering, A. W. "Introduction." In A. W. Chickering and Associates, *The Modern American College: Responding to the New Realities of Diverse Students and a Changing Society*. San Francisco: Jossey-Bass, 1981.

Collard, S., and Law, M. "The Limits of Perspective Transformation: A Critique of Mezirow's Theory." *Adult Education Quarterly*, 1989, *39* (2), 99–107.

Daloz, L. *Effective Teaching and Mentoring: Realizing the Transformational Power of Adult Learning Experiences*. San Francisco: Jossey-Bass, 1986.

Daloz, L. "Slouching Toward Bethlehem." *Continuing Higher Education*, 1990, *39* (1), 2–9.

Freire, P. *Pedagogy of the Oppressed*. New York: Seabury, 1970.

Freire, P. *Education for Critical Consciousness*. New York: Seabury, 1973.

Halterman, W. J. *The Complete Guide to Nontraditional Education*. New York: Facts on File, 1983.

Hamilton, E., and Cunningham, P. M. "Community-Based Adult Education." In S. B. Merriam and P. M. Cunningham (eds.), *Handbook of Adult and Continuing Education*. San Francisco: Jossey-Bass, 1989.

Hurley, M. E. "Empowering Adult Learners." *Adult Learning*, 1991, *2* (4), 20–27.

Merriam, S. B., and Caffarella, R. S. *Learning in Adulthood: A Comprehensive Guide*. San Francisco: Jossey-Bass, 1991.

Mezirow, J. D. "A Critical Theory of Adult Learning and Education." *Adult Education Quarterly*, 1981, *32* (1), 3–24.

Mezirow, J. D. "A Critical Theory of Self-Directed Learning." In S. D. Brookfield (ed.), *Self-Directed Learning: From Theory to Practice*. New Directions for Adult and Continuing Education, no. 25. San Francisco: Jossey-Bass, 1985.

Mezirow, J. D. "Transformation Theory and Social Action: A Response to Collard and Law." *Adult Education Quarterly*, 1989, *39* (3), 170–176.

Mezirow, J. "Conclusion: Toward Transformative Learning and Emancipatory Education." In J. Mezirow and Associates, *Fostering Critical Reflection in Adulthood: A Guide to Transformative and Emancipatory Learning*. San Francisco: Jossey-Bass, 1990a.

Mezirow, J. "How Critical Reflection Triggers Transformative Learning." In J. Mezirow and Associates, *Fostering Critical Reflection in Adulthood: A Guide to Transformative and Emancipatory Learning*. San Francisco: Jossey-Bass, 1990b.

Mezirow, J. *Transformative Dimensions of Adult Learning*. San Francisco: Jossey-Bass, 1991.

Mezirow, J., and Associates. *Fostering Critical Reflection in Adulthood: A Guide to Transformative and Emancipatory Learning*. San Francisco: Jossey-Bass, 1990.

Rogers, C. "The Foundations of the Person-Centered Approach." *Education*, 1979, *100* (2), 98–107.

M. CAROLYN CLARK is assistant professor of adult education in the Department of Educational Human Resource Development, Texas A&M University, College Station.

A framework of levels, states, and structures of consciousness is offered and challenges are put forth in an effort to expand the context for the study and practice of adult learning. Modern science and "ancient wisdom" are complementary knowledge sources.

Consciousness and Learning: New and Renewed Approaches

Marcie Boucouvalas

When the 1972 Nobel Prize winners in physics and chemistry were asked for what the awards in their fields may be given in the year 2000, both unequivocally answered that it would be for the study of human consciousness, an area that they construed as the new frontier (Green and Green, 1977). Over twenty years have now passed and the new millennium is upon us. Fields as diverse as physics, the neurological sciences, theology, psychology, anthropology, and ecology are reconsidering the enigma of human consciousness, an arena that has intrigued humanity down through the ages. The concept of consciousness is now slowly being revived also in the literature and lexicon of learning, following a hiatus of decades since William James ([1902] 1913, p. 518) wrote that "the whole drift of my education goes to persuade me that the world of our present consciousness is only one out of many worlds of consciousness that exist, and that those other worlds must contain experiences that have a meaning for our lives also."

Usage of the term *consciousness* is becoming increasingly frequent in the literature on learning. As a concept, however, consciousness is still difficult and thorny and may well frustrate those looking for conceptual precision. In fact, there are those who urge us to abandon use of the term altogether (for example, Wilkes, 1984). Between the extremes of complete abandonment and indiscriminate, uncritical use lies the territory of exploratory consideration. Accordingly, this chapter invites the reader to consider how the growing literature base on human consciousness can be organized and sorted out in a meaningful way so as to provide an expanded context for understanding adult learning in theory and practice.

NEW DIRECTIONS FOR ADULT AND CONTINUING EDUCATION, no. 57, Spring 1993   © Jossey-Bass Publishers

Whether explicitly or implicitly, the amorphous literature related to consciousness and learning affords a guiding image of what a human is or could become. The streams of thought converging under this rubric share the perspective put forth decades ago by Berger and Luckmann (1966) that human consciousness is constructed with the aid of society and culture but too often is taken to represent the whole rather than one part or dimension of reality. While cultural, linguistic, and individual factors create one's reality, many other modes of consciousness are available, and consciousness can be deconstructed, that is, the structures can be made apparent to enable fuller development of oneself. The literature on consciousness and learning rests on a deeper, wider, and more expanded and integrated vision of self. Many ways of knowing are acknowledged—some that we may not understand as yet, some that involve modes other than the senses or the intellect. In this vein, Western science and "ancient wisdom" from Eastern philosophies to Native American practices together offer a promising partnership in the depiction of human phenomena.

Ancient Wisdom and Native Knowing: A Complement to Modern Science

While neuroscientists (and engineers working with them) are heralding unprecedented technological advances in understanding the structure and function of our cognitive capacities, anthropologists are renewing efforts to understand indigenous ways of knowing that have relevance to all humanity. An understanding of consciousness and learning is an integral part of these efforts. The Association for the Study of the Anthropology of Consciousness is leading the efforts in this regard. The field of adult education is likewise illuminating indigenous knowledge, as evidenced by *Indigenous Knowledge and Learning* (1992), a recent issue of the journal *Convergence*. It seems timely that 1993 has been designated as the International Year of Indigenous People.

A resurgence of indigenous ways of knowing is witnessed around the world as cultural groups (some previously oppressed, some rediscovering their roots, and some maintaining their lives as usual) are recognizing and respecting their native ways of knowing, many of which involve a variety of states of consciousness. For example, when Pamela Colorado, an Oneida Indian, was completing her doctoral dissertation at Harvard University, she had difficulty communicating in the way that was expected. This turbulent trial led her to the realization that not only did Native American people look at life differently, but "even the way we come to knowledge and present that knowledge is totally different from the Western way. . . . It's almost as if we have a science of our own! Our religion and our spirituality are built into our science" (Colorado, 1992, pp. 19–20).

These revelations led her to found the Worldwide Indigenous Science

Network, which nonindigenous people are also invited to join. Perhaps as many peoples around the world rediscover their traditions, an emphasis on cultural differences will be complemented by a discovery of common dynamics of human consciousness and its relation to learning.

Bean (1992) observed commonalities among tribal cultures around the globe vis-à-vis their consciousness, their sense of unity and community, their way of living in an interconnected web with other living forms, their deep spirituality—all of which are modes of consciousness that the deep ecology movement is currently calling for (Fox, 1990a, 1990b; Roszak, 1992) and are consonant with what physicist David Bohm (1973, 1980) calls the implicate order of the universe. His research reveals two orders: the explicate and the implicate. The explicate is how the world appears unfolded before our senses, a world of separate entities perceived in ordinary personal consciousness. Enfolded within the explicate is the implicate order, a more subtle fundamental arrangement to the universe, a world of interconnectedness perceived in transpersonal consciousness where one's identity transcends the individual self. Ecologically, this transpersonal consciousness enables one to perceive one's commonality with all living creatures and thus protect the environment as motivated from the inside, not just from a feeling of moral obligation emanating from externally given "shoulds" and "oughts." Discussions on the nature of this aspect of consciousness are also found in the literature of many religious and spiritual traditions (see, for example, Tart, 1991) and are further illuminated by physicists who have made their research accessible to the nonphysicist (Zukav, 1979; Capra, 1987, 1989, 1991; Capra, Steindl-Rast, and Matus, 1991). These are some examples of how modern science and "ancient wisdoms" are complementary sources of knowledge regarding consciousness and learning.

A Framework of Levels, States, and Structures

One way of organizing the literature on consciousness is to think in terms of levels, states, and structures of consciousness. An implicit claim in the literature is that a wide range of "awarenesses" is available to humanity and that changes can be experienced and movement made among levels, states, and structures of consciousness, although the latter implies development of a fairly lasting nature. The semantics of organizing and labeling these three arenas is a bit treacherous since the terms themselves are used in a variety of ways in the literature. More important is an understanding that shifts in consciousness can indicate a quantitative measure (level) or a qualitative state, both of which are temporary, or shifts can reflect a more lasting developmental nature (structures and processes). Not only are adults capable of learning how to shift consciousness, but what is learned, how it is learned, and the perspective of the learner change with the various shifts. Foremost, the differences between levels and states of consciousness are important.

Levels. Levels of consciousness, in technological terms at least, can be defined with respect to the degree to which one's awareness is geared externally or internally, as depicted in Figure 6.1 by the number of cycles per second emitted from the brain. Beta level may be considered ordinary awake consciousness, the alert attention with which we are most familiar. Movement to an even more externally focused consciousness is called gamma. One's field of vision narrows as in the expression "blind with rage." It is thought that murders of passion are committed while in "gamma level." A learning-related example is the kind of anxiety that interferes with learning, as in "blanking out" on a test. Tunnel vision occurs in gamma due to an overfocus on the target and an accompanying loss of one's field of vision.

Conversely, movement toward a more balanced awareness (inner/ outer) is heralded with alpha, relaxed diffuse attention where one's focus becomes more inward in nature. Theta, on the borderline between waking and sleeping, is increasingly viewed as a level where creative problem solving can take place. Theta is usually short-lived as one drops off to sleep or is jarred into ordinary waking consciousness by an alarm clock. Some corporations, however, are training executives and others how to linger longer in theta. Finally, delta, encompassing the slowest brain wave frequencies, is associated with deep sleep, coma, and the like, where consciousness is sufficiently withdrawn from external focus so that one appears "unaware," although the degree of awareness of and communica-

Figure 6.1. Brain Rhythms or Levels of Consciousness and Corresponding Brain Wave Frequencies

Brain Rhythm		Brain Wave Frequency	
Gamma:	agitation	26–40 cps	↑
Beta:	concentration attention	13–26 cps	Attention focused on outside world
Alpha:	restful diffuse attention	8–13 cps	
Theta:	drowsy reverie creative insight deep meditation	4–8 cps	Attention withdrawn from surroundings and focused on inside world
Delta:	deep sleep coma	.5–4 cps	↓

Note: Brain wave frequencies expressed in cycles per second (cps).

tion with the external world is still at issue (for example, the literature on how much one can actually hear and perceive during anaesthesia; see Miletich, 1988).

Studies by Kamiya (1971) showed that individuals could learn to move from one brain wave frequency to another with training, thus paving the way for biofeedback training, about which volumes have now been written. Many kinds of feedback devices are being developed, and some are paired with computer imaging approaches. All give information back to individuals to help them practice self-regulation of biological processes. For example, an external signal (light or sound) indicates the wavelength emitted, and individuals learn to produce and vary the signal by fine-tuning their consciousness of the inner feeling associated with each frequency. When the external cue is withdrawn, it is hoped that the individual can voluntarily choose and enter the level of consciousness desired. One consistent finding suggests that external assistance provided by biofeedback data helps some individuals ultimately reach states common to yogi meditators. Some educators (for example, Roberts, 1989) consider this ability to choose one's consciousness level and enter and exit at will a hallmark of the educated person for the twenty-first century.

States. Whatever the level of consciousness, however, the qualitative state may differ. For example, delta could indicate deep sleep or coma. Theta could reflect a hypnotic state, a meditative state, or that twilight state between waking and sleeping (hypnagogic) and sleeping and waking (hypnopompic). Each state of consciousness provides its own picture of reality. A state of consciousness is basically a major alteration in the way that the mind functions. More specifically, each state of consciousness has a unique configuration (system) of ten subsystems that form a unique pattern (Tart, 1972, 1975). For example, one subsystem is the space-time sense. Sense of time and parameters of space may seem expanded or contracted in different states. Another subsystem is one's sense of identity, which can range in different states from small and restricted to a more expanded sense of relatedness with the cosmos. As Tart (1972, 1975) emphasizes, however, we need to know more about how each subsystem changes for each specific state of consciousness.

An important corollary is the concept of state specificity of knowledge. This means not only that some things are learned best in a specific state of consciousness but also that individuals may not be able to understand or explain how they arrived at a particular understanding or meaning or may have difficulty communicating at least verbally to a person in another state. Educators attempting to better study and understand learning in a specific state may need to enter that territory themselves.

There are meditative states, hypnotic and autohypnotic states, reverie, and many others as yet unnamed. Krippner (1972) has suggested that as many as twenty-two different states are possible. The burgeoning literature in this area focuses both on understanding different states of consciousness and on changing one's consciousness. A variety of triggers can induce movement to and through different levels and states of consciousness. Some pathways are new due to the advent of technological advances, others are renewed versions of more classical approaches. Some are construed as techniques to deliberately induce change, others as merely catalysts to a more incremental process of moving through consciousness. An often tacit assumption is the vital connection between mind and body. The literature teems with discussion of meditation, hypnosis and autosuggestion, guided imagery and visualization, lucid dreams, somatic disciplines, trance states, including the ultradian rhythms or everyday trances (see Rossi, 1986) and various other states. Although it is outside the scope of this chapter to review and evaluate the myriad of pathways, the discussions of Ferguson (1980), Roberts (1989), and Hansen and Gueulette (1988) on psychotechnologies are recommended, as well as Maxfield's (1990) review on "whole mind learning."

The states-of-consciousness literature sheds light on the experience that what is usually not part of awareness in ordinary waking consciousness may indeed come into awareness in other states. Different levels and states of consciousness often provide glimpses into other "worlds of consciousness." Movement, however, from glimpses to an ontology or manner of being in the world is at the crux of the structures of consciousness, a developmental phenomenon.

Structures. Beyond levels and states is a very different kind of shift in consciousness that is more lasting. Futurists even predict an evolution of consciousness based on a progressive transformation of its structures. Structures are foundational; they form the context of consciousness that holds the content. While some may argue with the term *structures,* I emphasize the progressive movement toward an expanded, more developed sense of self in both its autonomous and homonomous dimensions (that is, the self as a unique individual and as part of a greater whole).

The literature on adult cognition refers to movement from dichotomous (either/or), to relativistic (contextual), to dialectical thinking where multiple realities or things previously seen as antithetical can be understood as parts of greater wholes. Likewise, moral development moves from an egocentric orientation to an embracing of universal ethical principles, whereas social cognition unfolds from egocentric to societal perspective taking. Progressive unfolding of the human experience entails movement toward more complexity, greater awareness, and less egocentric egocentrism. Transpersonal models of development (that is, our understanding of development beyond ego) are especially meaningful in affording greater understanding, whether one is inclined toward the structural-hierarchical orientation of Wilber (for a concise yet comprehensive treatment, see

Wilber, 1981; Wilber, Engler, and Brown, 1986) or the dynamic-dialectical orientation of Washburn (1988). Movement beyond a purely "what is in it for me" level of motivation and development to an expanded sense of identity connecting with other creatures in the cosmos define the kind of shift in consciousness that may be useful in solving the world's problems.

Practical Applications and Theory Building

Shifts in the structures of consciousness have been called for to deal with the world challenges of today and tomorrow. If, however, processes such as meditation are out of reach for whatever reason, what then? Looking to the future, Murphy (1992) offers an encyclopedic overview of what he calls "transformative practices" available to all people, from spiritually oriented practice to somatic disciplines, and others. Some individuals are exploring on their own paths, others in groups, mostly in nonformal education settings. Murphy's analysis of evidence from a wide range of disciplines points to the possibility of a further evolution of consciousness based on the currently latent abilities residing in consciousness, which he calls "transformative capacities." He emphasizes, however, the importance of balancing transformative practice with ethical awareness and wisdom.

One area not noted by Murphy (1992) is the powerful role that intimate relationships play as pathways of further development of one's structures of consciousness (Lilly and Lilly, 1976; Gibb, 1978; Campbell, 1980; Welwood, 1990). Other kinds of relationships are relevant as well. Good mentors and learning facilitators, effective managers, and skilled consultants might be challenged to pursue this literature and reflect on the developmental potential of interpersonal relationships. Entrepreneurs such as Robert Schwartz of Tarrytown, New York, engage in management development practices with an eye toward contributing to the evolution of consciousness. Human resources development efforts by practitioners such as Linda Morris, director of Industries Service Education at Ernst & Young, and Robert Haas, chief executive officer of Levi-Strauss, are also following this lead. These are but a few examples of how the older ideals of civilization are renewed today during our watershed period of profound societal transformation.

With regard to the literature on levels and states of consciousness, there are several arenas where the age-old and newer approaches converge. In cultures throughout history, people have ingested a variety of plants and other substances for ceremonial purposes. Enhanced mental functioning often resulted. Some cultures still engage in this process. In modern times, pharmaceuticals (which are either derived from plants or synthetically made) are employed in a variety of ways vis-à-vis consciousness and learning. For instance, beyond its deleterious "bad press" reports, LSD has been used for decades in controlled doses both for research purposes and as a therapeutic aid. As a result of such interventions, Stanley Grof has constructed models of the multilayered unconscious based on his observations that "LSD is an amplifier of mental processes that confronts the experiencer with his (her) own consciousness" (Grof, 1973, p. 17). In addition to psychoactive drugs (Lukoff, Zanger, and Lu, 1990), interventions include the successful administration of pharmaceuticals to dyslexics (Wilshner, 1986) and the role of specific agents in improving mental functioning, especially long- and short-term memory (for example, Blakemore, 1987; "Test Drug . . . ," 1986; Reisberg and others, 1983). Pharmaceutical intervention for enhanced mental functioning is emerging as a major topic of debate (Roberts, 1990).

Another example of the convergence of old and new pathways is music. Since the time of Pythagoras, music has been recognized as important to inducing different states of consciousness; and from a theological orientation, music in certain octaves has prepared one for prayer and connection with spirit down through the ages. Bonny and Savery (1973) developed a systematic means to move individuals through various experiences of consciousness by listening to an organized selection of mostly classical pieces. Music is also a basis for the Bulgarian Lozanov approach to the learning of suggestopedia (the science of suggestion applied to learning), which has been applied to language learning in particular (Lozanov, 1978). A minimum of an alpha level of consciousness is required, induced, and maintained by this approach. The Society for Accelerated Learning and Teaching, a movement founded in the United States, is also based on the Lozanov approach. The theory of suggestion, the basis for these approaches, is also the basis for the advent of subliminal technology, where learning is purportedly outside conscious awareness.

Research on the subliminal is part of a growing literature base on learning without conscious awareness. Subliminal perception refers to one's ability to register, process, and act on information received below the level of conscious awareness. This perceptual threshold varies within and among individuals as a result of stress, environment, and other influences. Cultures can nurture perceptual expansion or diminution. The notion of subliminal perception is based on the idea that while some communications cannot be perceived through ordinary consciousness, they may be registered subliminally. The first scholarly attempts to examine this territory were made in the late 1800s by Myers (1976), and the effort continues in modern research (Shevrin and Dickman, 1980). Subliminal communication technology has become increasingly sophisticated and available for popular consumption, including information on how to create one's own programs. Audiocassettes, videotapes, as well as microcomputer-television connections, which through visual or auditory means, or both, transmit subliminal messages during otherwise ordinary television programs, all offer promise and benefit to adult learning, as well as potential perils in their deceptive or surreptitious use (Boucouvalas, 1990a, 1990b).

Research findings pertaining to the effectiveness of subliminal technology (especially self-help tapes) on learning seem inconclusive, ranging from claims of failure (National Research Council, 1991) to claims of success, which seem to depend on how open individuals are to suggestion. Cognitive structure and style (J. Moore, 1982; D. Moore, 1988), brain hemisphericity (Charman, 1979; Pajurkova-Flannery, 1979; Gur, Packer, and Sackeim, 1977; Shifren, 1982), and personality (Kotz and Miler, 1991) have all been related to one's susceptibility to subliminal suggestion. According to the findings of Schulman, Schulman, and Rafferty (1990), however, who conducted in-depth comparative research on a spectrum of marketed products, the effectiveness of subliminal learning depends on the quality of the tapes and how they are produced. Particularly effective, it seems, is the "high-technology" tape whose script is written positively, which stimulates alpha or theta waves, and whose message is in stereo, that is, employs multiple channels for messages. Their findings on stereo messages are consistent with the "multiple-channels" position of consciousness supported by Dennett (1991), a well-known researcher and writer on the mind and brain. Help is offered by Schulman, Schulman, and Rafferty (1990) as to how one can test the quality of such products.

Essentially, the existence of nonconscious learning is no longer at issue (see Loftus, 1992, on the topic of unconscious cognition). Attention is now being focused on the depth, breadth, and quality of mental processes involved. There are ongoing debates in the arena of foreign language learning about the role that unconscious processes play in language acquisition (see, for example, McLaughlin, 1990; Schmidt, 1990).

In general, then, the literature on consciousness and learning has much to offer both practice and theory building in adult learning, but an identifiable knowledge base for the field has yet to be synthesized. Wacks (1987) has urged us to think in terms of self-transcendence as a purpose of adult education. Hansen and Gueulette (1988) afford a comprehensive understanding of a variety of psychotechnologies for changing consciousness. Maxfield (1990) offers an overview of the "whole mind" movement with adult learners. And Henry (1988) proposes a model of transformative learning that goes beyond levels and states to take into account structures of human consciousness. For Freire (1973), consciousness and learning entail the development of an awareness of one's oppression and empowerment to take action. For Mezirow (1991), consciousness and learning mean becoming aware of and transforming one's perspective, which is composed of meaning structures similar to the structures of consciousness. His research has contributed greatly to our understanding of reflection on the contents of consciousness, particularly in the critical, rational manner that he calls "critical reflectivity."

The literature on consciousness and learning reviewed in this chapter complements these efforts by acknowledging ways of knowing beyond the rational and the analytical and by considering contemplative reflection on the structures of consciousness so as to observe and understand not just one's thoughts (that is, assumptions and values) but also the structure or context that enables some thoughts and perhaps impedes others. Toward this end, Boyd and Myers (1988), writing from a Jungian perspective, consider the process of discernment, rather than critical reflection, as a vehicle to what they call "transformative education," although they tend not to broach the issue of different levels and states of consciousness or of pathways to catalyze the process. Discernment is an inner journey toward and dialogue with the unconscious. One must first be receptive or open to information that surfaces, then recognize and acknowledge its relevance, and, finally, grieve the disintegration of prior structures and ways of knowing in order to move on. All of us as practitioners of life can continue to explore, both within ourselves as well as with our clients and colleagues, an experiential understanding of a deeper, more expanded self, whether as temporary levels and states or, developmentally, as structures of consciousness.

Consciousness and Adult Learning: Toward the New Millennium

This chapter offers only a rudimentary exploration of the multifaceted arena of consciousness and learning, a territory that, at minimum, expands our understanding of what learning and knowing encompass. A variety of material resources have been offered for further inquiry and a range of ideas put forth for reflection as we move adult learning into the twenty-first century. The facilitation of adult learning, program development, administration, and other arenas are insufficiently addressed by ordinary beta-level consciousness alone. We need adult learners and educators who understand and function at a fuller capacity from a wide range of levels and states of consciousness and who can choose to engage one over another for specific types of learning.

As the twenty-first century approaches, practitioners and researchers are challenged to explore this expanded context for adult learning in both theory and practice. To the extent that we are able to accomplish this feat, we are preparing for the new millennium.

References

Bean, W. "Reflections on a Consultation on the Development of Tribals in Asia." *Convergence,* 1992, 25 (1), 5–17.

Berger, P. L., and Luckmann, T. *The Social Construction of Reality: A Treatise in the Sociology of Knowledge.* New York: Doubleday, 1966.

Blakemore, C. B. "Cyclandelate in the Treatment of Multi-Infarct Dementia: Interim Findings from a Multi-Centre Study in General Practice." *Drugs,* 1987, *33* (supplement 2), 110–113.

Bohm, D. "Quantum Theory as an Indicator of a New Order in Physics. Part B: Implicate and Explicate Order in Physical Law." *Foundations of Physics,* 1973, *3* (2), 139–168.

Bohm, D. *Wholeness and the Implicate Order.* New York: Routledge & Kegan Paul, 1980.

Bonny, H. L., and Savery, L. M. *Music and Your Mind: Listening with a New Consciousness.* New York: HarperCollins, 1973.

Boucouvalas, M. "Learning Without Conscious Awareness: The Subliminal as a Case-in-Point." In W. Rivera (ed.), *Proceedings of the Lifelong Learning Research Conference.* College Park: University of Maryland, 1990a.

Boucouvalas, M. "Subliminal Technology and the Adult Learner: Contributions, Caveats, and Concerns." In *Proceedings of the National Conference on the Adult Learner.* Columbia: University of South Carolina, 1990b.

Boyd, R. D., and Myers, J. G. "Transformative Education." *International Journal of Lifelong Education,* 1988, *7* (4), 261–284.

Campbell, S. *The Couple's Journey: Intimacy as a Path to Wholeness.* San Luis Obispo, Calif.: Impact, 1980.

Capra, F. *The Turning Point.* New York: Bantam, 1987.

Capra, F. *Uncommon Wisdom.* New York: Bantam, 1989.

Capra, F. *The Tao of Physics.* (3rd. ed.) Boston: Shambhala, 1991.

Capra, F., Steindl-Rast, D., and Matus, T. *Belonging to the Universe: Explorations on the Frontiers of Science and Spirituality.* New York: HarperCollins, 1991.

Charman, D. K. "An Examination of Relationship Between Subliminal Perception, Visual Information Processing, Levels of Processing, and Hemispheric Asymmetries." *Perceptual and Motor Skills,* 1979, *49* (2), 451–455.

Colorado, P. "Wayfaring and the New Sun: Indigenous Science in the Modern World." *Noetic Sciences Review,* 1992, *22,* 19–23.

Dennett, D. C. *Consciousness Explained.* Boston: Little, Brown, 1991.

Ferguson, M. *The Aquarian Conspiracy.* Los Angeles: Tarcher, 1980.

Fox, W. *Toward a Transpersonal Ecology: Developing New Foundations for Environmentalism.* Boston: Shambhala, 1990a.

Fox, W. "Transpersonal Ecology: Psychologizing Ecophilosophy." *Journal of Transpersonal Psychology,* 1990b, *22* (1), 59–96.

Freire, P. *Education for Critical Consciousness.* New York: Seabury, 1973.

Gibb, J. *Trust: A New View of Personal and Organizational Development.* Los Angeles: Guild of Tutors Press, 1978.

Green, F., and Green, A. *Beyond Biofeedback.* New York: Dell, 1977.

Grof, S. "Theoretical and Empirical Basis of Transpersonal Psychology: Observations from LSD Research." *Journal of Transpersonal Psychology,* 1973, *5* (1), 15–54.

Gur, R. C., Packer, I. K., and Sackeim, H. A. "Hemisphericity, Cognitive Set, and Susceptibility to Subliminal Perception." *Journal of Abnormal Psychology,* 1977, *86* (6), 624–630.

Hansen, C., and Gueulette, D. G. "Psychotechnology as Instructional Technology: Systems for a Deliberate Change of Consciousness." *Educational Communication and Technology Journal,* 1988, *36* (4), 231–242.

Henry, J. "Development and Learning for Transformation: A Model Linking Lifelong Learning and Transpersonal Psychology." Unpublished doctoral dissertation, Department of Adult Education, University of Georgia, 1988.

Indigenous Knowledge and Learning. Special issue of *Convergence,* 1992, *25* (entire issue 1).

James, W. *The Varieties of Religious Experience: A Study in Human Nature.* White Plains, N.Y.: Longman, 1913. (Originally published 1902.)

Kamiya, J. *Biofeedback and Self-Control.* Hawthorne, N.Y.: Aldine, 1971.

Kotz, H. F., and Miler, A. T. "Subliminal Stimulation, Choice Behavior, and Some Personality Correlates of Subliminal Sensitivity." *Perceptual and Motor Skills,* 1991, *72,* 315–322.

Krippner, S. "Altered States of Consciousness." In J. White (ed.), *The Highest State of Consciousness.* New York: Doubleday, 1972.

Lilly, J., and Lilly, A. *The Dyadic Cyclone: Autobiography of a Couple.* New York: Simon & Schuster, 1976.

Loftus, E. F. (ed.). *Science Watch.* Special section of *American Psychologist,* 1992, *47* (6), 760–800.

Lozanov, G. *Suggestology and Outlines of Suggestopedy.* (M. Hall-Pozharlieva and K. Pashmakova, trans.) New York: Gordon and Beach, 1978.

Lukoff, D., Zanger, R., and Lu, F. "Transpersonal Psychology Research Review: Psychoactive Substances and Transpersonal States." *Journal of Transpersonal Psychology,* 1990, *22* (2), 107–148.

McLaughlin, B. " 'Conscious' Versus 'Unconscious' Learning." *TESOL Quarterly,* 1990, *24* (4), 617–634.

Maxfield, D. G. "Learning with the Whole Mind." In R. M. Smith and Associates, *Learning to Learn Across the Life Span.* San Francisco: Jossey-Bass, 1990.

Mezirow, J. *Transformative Dimensions of Adult Learning.* San Francisco: Jossey-Bass, 1991.

Miletich, J. *States of Awareness: An Annotated Bibliography.* New York: Greenwood, 1988.

Moore, D. M. "Cognitive Style and Subliminal Instruction." In *Proceedings of Selected Research Papers Presented at the Annual Meeting of the Association for Educational Communications and Technology.* New Orleans: Association for Educational Communications and Technology, 1988. (ED 295 653).

Moore, J. S. "An Exploratory Study of Subliminal Perception and Field Dependence in a Concept Learning Task Taught by Television." Unpublished doctoral dissertation, College of Education, Virginia Polytechnic Institute and State University, 1982.

Murphy, M. *The Future of the Body: Explorations into the Further Evolution of Human Nature.* Los Angeles: Tarcher, 1992.

Myers, F.W.H. *The Subliminal Consciousness.* New York: Arno, 1976.

National Research Council. *In the Mind's Eye: Enhancing Human Performance.* Washington, D.C.: National Academy Press, 1991.

Pajurkova-Flannery, E. M. "Subliminal Perception in the Context of Functional Hemispheric Asymmetries." *Dissertation Abstracts International,* 1979, *40* (4B), 1870.

Reisberg, B., and others. "Effects of Naloxine in Senile Dementia: Double-Blind Trial." *New England Journal of Medicine,* 1983, *308,* 721–722.

Roberts, T. B. "Multistate Education: Metacognitive Implications of the Mind/Body Psychotechnologies." *Journal of Transpersonal Psychology,* 1989, *21* (1), 83–102.

Roberts, T. B. "Cognitive Science, Religion, and Academic Freedom vs. the Drug Prohibition Ideology." In A. S. Treback and K. B. Zeese (eds.), *The Great Issues of Drug Policy.* Washington, D.C.: Drug Policy Foundation, 1990.

Rossi, E. L. "Altered States of Consciousness in Everyday Life: Ultradian Rhythms." In B. B. Wolman and M. Ullman (eds.), *Handbook of States of Consciousness.* New York: Van Nostrand Reinhold, 1986.

Roszak, T. *The Voice of the Earth.* New York: Simon & Schuster, 1992.

Schmidt R. W. "The Role of Consciousness in Second Language Learning." *Applied Linguistics,* 1990, *11* (2), 129–158.

Schulman, L. M., Schulman, J., and Rafferty, G. P. *Subliminal: The New Challenge to Personal Power.* Santa Monica, Calif.: Info Books, 1990.

Shevrin, H., and Dickman, S. "The Psychological Unconscious: A Necessary Assumption for All Psychological Theory." *American Psychologist,* 1980, *35* (5), 421–435.

Shifren, I. W. "The Interaction Between Hemispheric Preference and the Perception of Subliminal Auditory and Visual Symbiotic Gratification Stimuli." *Dissertation Abstracts International,* 1982, *42* (10B), 4211–4212.

Tart, C. T. "States of Consciousness and State-Specific Sciences." *Science,* 1972, *176,* 1203–1210.

Tart, C. T. *States of Consciousness.* New York: Dutton, 1975.

Tart, C. T. (ed.). *Transpersonal Psychologies: Perspectives on the Mind from Seven Great Spiritual Traditions.* (3rd ed.) New York: HarperCollins, 1991.

"Test Drug Seems to Improve Alzheimer's Disease." *Drug Topics,* 1986, *130,* 38, 42.

Wacks, V. Q. "A Case for Self-Transcendence as a Purpose of Adult Education." *Adult Education Quarterly,* 1987, *38,* 46–55.

Washburn, M. *The Ego and the Dynamic Ground: A Transpersonal Theory of Human Development.* Albany: State University of New York Press, 1988.

Welwood, J. "Intimate Relationship as Path." *Journal of Transpersonal Psychology,* 1990, *22* (1), 51–58.

Wilber, K. *Up from Eden: A Transpersonal View of Human Evolution.* Boston: Shambhala, 1981.

Wilber, K., Engler, J., and Brown, D. P. *Transformations of Consciousness: Conventional and Contemplative Perspectives on Development.* Boston: Shambhala, 1986.

Wilkes, K. "Is Consciousness Important?" *British Journal of Philosophical Sciences,* 1984, *35,* 223–243.

Wilshner, C. R. "The Nootropic Concept and Dyslexia." *Annals of Dyslexia,* 1986, *36,* 118–137.

Zukav, G. *The Dancing Wu Li Masters: An Overview of the New Physics.* New York: Morrow, 1979.

MARCIE BOUCOUVALAS is associate professor of adult education at the Graduate Center of Virginia Polytechnic Institute and State University, Falls Church.

Learning and knowing are integrally and inherently situated in the everyday world of human activity. The promise of situated cognition lies in providing a more accurate understanding of how adults learn.

The Promise of Situated Cognition

Arthur L. Wilson

What does it mean for cognition to be situated? To begin with a practical grounding, let us look at an example.

On a recent family trip by automobile across the American West, my wife, daughter, and I needed to be constantly engaged in the activity of navigating our journey. This turned out to be more than a simple matter of following some lines on one of our many maps. To start, prior to each day's departure, we would all huddle around a pile of open maps, tourist brochures, "trip tiks," and various other travel and tourist advisories to discuss our potential travel goals for that particular day. Our discussions always included questions such as "How far do we want to go today?" "What do we want to see along the way?" "How much time can we spend here and still get there?" Seemingly, once discussed and planned, our itinerary would be set for the day. Not so. Throughout the day, all of our travel information would be in constant use as our traveling brought us new information; we thought about it and then made decisions about what to do. Likewise, the driver, who was responsible for the mechanical portion of the travel, was very dependent on the other two for counsel and direction, which often required extended discussions on what the maps meant and how they related to our actual driving. And, in a very fascinating way, it was often the actual driving on the roads that helped us to understand the maps that we were using. All of this navigating, of course, occurred in a constant atmosphere of talk as we individually and collectively examined our travel information and proposed various options. Important to this topic as well, our understanding of our actions was constantly changing as we interacted with this particular set of circumstances. Thus, our learning, knowing, and understanding in this very

NEW DIRECTIONS FOR ADULT AND CONTINUING EDUCATION, no. 57, Spring 1993 © Jossey-Bass Publishers

mundane activity was fundamentally structured by our interactions with each other and with the elements of the circumstances, the maps, roads, tourist attractions, and other conditions of road travel.

The point of beginning with this story is to suggest that context is not just an important element in thinking about human learning but is perhaps central to our understanding of adult cognition. Thus, the example illustrates some of the ingredients of context and how they affect knowing and learning. First is the notion that learning and thinking in the everyday world are typically social activities; for example, my family's planning of our journey was fundamentally structured by our constant interpersonal interaction. Second, adults' ability to think and learn are profoundly structured by the availability of situationally provided "tools." Finally, human thinking is profoundly structured by interaction with the setting. My family's trip constantly changed as we were engaged with the activity of traveling. Thus, to appreciate the significance of context, we have to recognize the importance of thinking and learning in authentic activities. That is, to understand the central place of context in thinking and learning, we have to recognize that cognition is a social activity that incorporates the mind, the body, the activity, and the ingredients of the setting in a complex interactive and recursive manner (Rogoff and Lave, 1984; Lave, 1988).

To explore this issue of how context structures knowing and learning, I examine here some of the arguments for this point of view, review how adult educators have dealt with the notion of learning and its relation to experience, and, finally, suggest ideas for locating adult learning in what is referred to as authentic activity (Brown, Collins, and Duguid, 1989). Thus, I argue that adult education, which has often favored an experiential basis for learning, needs to more firmly situate its practice in the actual activities that require adult learning.

Does Learning Transfer Across Contexts?

Many of the models of adult learning are firmly rooted in a psychological orientation to learning (Rubenson, 1989). In this view, learning is an individual and internal mental process in which knowledge is acquired and stored for use at will in any circumstance. As Lave (1988, p. 4) has argued in her research of how adults do arithmetic (arguably the most transferable and decontextualized of all knowledge) in actual settings, "Conventional academic and folk theory assumes that arithmetic is learned in school . . . and is then literally carried away from school to be applied at will in any situation that calls for calculation." Brown, Collins, and Duguid (1989, p. 32) offered a similar analysis: In their view, education has assumed "a separation between knowing and doing, treating knowledge as an integral, self-sufficient substance, theoretically independent of the situations in which it is learned and used." This central conception of knowledge as transferable has dominated many of our theories of learning. But some research suggests that this conception may not be valid.

In a review of research on learning transfer, Lave (1988, p. 43) concluded that "the examples discussed here provide no empirical evidence concerning problem solving as it unfolds in action in everyday settings." In other words, the decontextualized study of problem solving in laboratories does not provide evidence for verifying the assumption of transferability, nor does it provide insight into how people think in the real world. Lave argued that the research on learning transfer has not focused on the right issues precisely because it has attempted to separate learning from the social world in which it occurs, thereby ignoring the contextual elements that give it meaning.

This is the central concern: "To assume that under ideal circumstances people's underlying capacities or processes can be attributed to their internal functioning without concern for the context of their activity is unrealistic" (Rogoff, 1984, p. 2). In other words, knowledge and learning do not easily transfer across contexts. Knowledge and learning have to be understood as inextricably integrated with the setting in which they occur. An understanding of adults' activity in a particular setting is central to an understanding of their learning; learning is thus "fundamentally situated" (Brown, Collins, and Duguid, 1989, p. 32).

What does it mean to be "fundamentally situated"? It means that "context is an integral aspect of cognitive events, not a nuisance variable" (Rogoff, 1984, p. 3). Learning is thus an everyday event that is social in nature because it occurs with other people; it is "tool dependent" because the setting provides mechanisms (computers, maps, measuring cups) that aid and, more important, structure the cognitive process; and, finally, it is the interaction with the setting itself in relation to its social and tool-dependent nature that determines the learning. Thus, learning is a recursive process in which adults act in and interact with context (Lave, 1988; Rogoff, 1984).

To understand learning and knowing, the intricacies of human activities in a specific setting must be understood because they fundamentally structure how that learning and knowing occur (Resnick, 1987). Without the setting and activity, we cannot understand the cognition. As further evidence, Lave (1988; see also Lave, Murtaugh, and de la Rocha, 1984) has reported extensively on her research of how adults use arithmetic in grocery shopping to argue this point of view. In that research, she demonstrated not only that adults do not use the mathematics taught them in school but also that the calculations that adults perform to make grocery item choices are fundamentally structured by the setting of the grocery store and the activity of shopping. For example, when adults' computations of comparison pricing were tested in the actual shopping for groceries in which shoppers used elements of the setting, they exhibited an astounding

98 percent error-free set of solutions. When tested by paper and pencil for the same computational concepts by using school-taught mathematics (such as ratios for comparing prices of different sizes of items), adults' error-free solutions were only 59 percent. As Lave, Murtaugh, and de la Rocha (1984, p. 77) argued, "The setting often serves as a calculating device." They proceeded to describe incidents of shoppers using the elements of the setting and the shopping activity to perform their calculations. For example, one shopper accurately determined an incorrectly marked product by comparing its weight-price relation with other similarly weighted products rather than computing the actual per pound cost and then checking it with that printed on the package (which is the solution that school-taught mathematics would have preferred). That is, the elements of the setting—the actual grocery items, not computational procedures—were used to check discrepancies. Thus, with respect to whether knowledge and learning can cross contexts, proponents of a view of cognition as inherently situated offer evidence that adult learning and knowing are profoundly structured by the context in which they occur.

Learning, Experience, and Adult Education

Adult educators, too, have been concerned with the relation between learning and activity. One of the philosophical and instructional foundations of twentieth-century adult education is a focus on experience as essential to learning. Dewey's (1938, p. 25) notions of education rest solidly on experience as a foundation for learning: "All genuine education comes about through experience." Lindeman (1926, pp. 6, 9) tied the meaning of adult education to experience: "The approach to adult education will be via the route of situations, not subjects" because "the resource of highest value is the learner's experience." This traditional emphasis on experience shows up fully articulated in Knowles's (1980) depiction of andragogy, in which experience is again proposed as the central ingredient of learning. It is here that Knowles makes his central claim that meaningful adult learning is associated with the everyday problems of adults in their social world.

Kolb (1984) provides one of the more recent expressions of the importance of experience to learning. In Kolb's model, which is depicted cyclically, learning has four components: concrete experiences, reflective observation, abstract conceptualization, and active experimentation. While Kolb maintains that learning can begin anywhere in the cycle, his model clearly has experience as two of its major phases. Jarvis (1987, p. 11), who elaborated on Kolb's model of reflection, argued that "learning is not just a psychological process that happens in splendid isolation from the world in which the learner lives, but that it is intimately related to the world and affected by it." As we have seen, this is a central tenet of the situated view of knowing and learning. Indeed, Jarvis, in attempting to claim a sociological imperative for the study of adult learning, locates much of his argument in similar premises regarding its culturally organized nature. In fact, his argument is "to highlight the fact that learning always occurs within a social context and that the learner is to some extent a social construct, so that learning should be regarded as a social phenomenon as well as an individualistic one" (1987, p. 15), which suggests Jarvis's implicit criticism of Kolb's model for its lack of a social dimension.

Nonetheless, despite Jarvis's concerns with the social aspects of learning, his model of learning and reflection "commences and concludes with the person of the learner" (1987, p. 37). Although he referred to the social construction of the person and elaborated on the relations between individuals and the culture in which experience impacts learning, learning for Jarvis (as well as for Dewey, Lindeman, Knowles, and Kolb) is still largely a process occurring in the individual. In other words, the "person," to use Jarvis's term, is fundamentally formed within the relations of the cultural setting in which that person exists and learns. But these "objectified" factors (for example, language, class relations, and social settings) merely impact the individual and affect the reflective process, acting as "secondary social influences" (Rogoff, 1984, p. 5). Thus, there is no sense of the recursive structuring proposed by the situated view because Jarvis still sees learning, which he described as a gap between "biography and experience" (1987, p. 94), as located in the learner rather than spread across the person acting with others in culturally organized settings. Thus, in traditional adult education attempts to embed learning in experience, experience is seen to produce psychological motivations for learning. In the situated view, experience becomes activity and takes on a much more dynamic relation to learning. Adults no longer learn from experience, they learn in it, as they act in situations and are acted upon by situations.

Schön (1983, 1987) has received continuing attention in adult education and is particularly noteworthy with respect to this discussion because he has been quite concerned with how professionals "know-in-action." Although he tends to neglect the interpersonally interactive dimensions of knowing and learning, he does articulate the intricate and essential connections of cognition in setting and activity. His research and theories about reflection-in-action fundamentally situate the most powerful knowledgeability of humans in the doing of activities, not the application of generalized principles to practice; in fact, his work is an explicit critique of the idea of knowledge transfer. In his view, learning occurs as professional practitioners engage the very activity of their profession in the everyday world. For example, Schön has extensively documented the differences between the preferred systematic procedural knowledge of technical rationality and the actual tacit theories-in-use of reflection-in-action used by practicing professionals. In other words, practitioners do not apply well-constructed theories to well-understood problems to produce predictable results. Professional practice, therefore, is not "instrumental problem solving made rigorous by the application of scientific theory and technique" (Schön, 1983, p. 21).

As an example in adult education, Pennington and Green (1976) have demonstrated how continuing educators in practice do not follow the well-ordered planning models described in the theoretical literature; their planning activities are a function of their interaction with their specific settings. In Schön's view, learning and knowing are a function of people acting in the setting in which the knowing and learning are produced. Schön, however, does not address the interpersonal dynamics of practice or its tool dependence, although both are implicit in his depictions of professionals' knowing-in-action.

Schön's work comes closest to providing a framework in adult education that accounts for the inherently situated nature of adult cognition. Even so, there are several problems with all of these attempts to locate learning and knowing in experience. The situated view argues that cognition exists in the relations *among* people acting in culturally organized settings; that is, learning and knowing are recursively structured by people interacting with each other in tool-dependent settings to solve real problems in the everyday world (Lave, 1988; Resnick, 1987; Wertsch, 1985). It is the very activity itself that structures and brings meaning to the knowing and learning; that is, knowing and learning do not exist independently of the activity (as the navigational and grocery shopping reports indicate). Thus, not only have these traditional views focused too much on individual internal cognition, they have done so at the expense of losing the situationally unique structuring effect of activity on cognition. Thus, the real failure of such psychologically framed understandings of cognition is that they are unable to specify, that is, make known, the actual nature of experience and activity and their effect on cognition. Part of the promise of situated cognition lies in providing a definition of situational elements that structure adult cognition in important ways. This raises an entirely different question with respect to education practice. That is, how can we "resituate" learning so that it regains its circumstantially bound meaning? The answer, according to the situated view, lies in authentic activity.

Authentic Activity: Implications for Adult Education

The point of this chapter is to argue that "thinking is intricately interwoven with the context of the problem to be solved" (Rogoff, 1984, p. 2). This challenge to the dominant view of cognition as independent of context requires the restructuring of adult education practice. If the philosophy, analysis, and evidence of situated cognition have credence, then the practice of adult education can no longer be solely located in the traditional paradigm of decontextualized process and principle. It has to be located in the real world of human activity. If learning and knowing are to be based on the actual cognitive practices of humans, then they have to be located in authentic activity.

What then is authentic activity? Given the argument of this analysis, authentic activity has to involve situations in which actual cognitive processes are required rather than the simulated processes typically demanded in schooling (Resnick, 1987). As Brown, Collins, and Duguid (1989) have demonstrated, knowing and learning "index" the world because they are "intricately a product of the activity in which they are produced" (p. 33). In their view, learning is a process of enculturation: If we are to learn, we must become embedded in the culture in which the knowing and learning have meaning; conceptual frameworks cannot be meaningfully removed from their settings or practitioners. Learning in this respect is a cultural phenomenon because people do not learn abstract, self-contained units of knowledge that they then apply to new situations. Rather, "from a very early age and throughout their lives, people, consciously and unconsciously, adopt the behavior and belief systems of new social groups. Given the chance to observe and practice in situ the behavior of members of culture, people pick up relevant jargon, imitate behavior, and gradually start to act in accordance with its norms" (Brown, Collins, and Duguid, 1989, p. 34). Authentic activity, then, as portrayed throughout this discussion, is best understood as ordinary cognitive practices that are situationally defined, tool dependent, and socially interactive.

Authentic activity therefore requires that learning and knowing always be located in the actual situations of their creation and use, not the simulations artificially constructed in schooling practices. Thus, learning and knowing are a process of enculturation, not simply a matter of acquisition. Problem solving and human cognitive practices are carried out in conjunction with the setting, not simply as internalized mental processes. Thus, proponents of this view offer various forms of apprenticeship as the crucial instructional mechanism for gaining the situational proficiency necessary to operate in the world: "Cognitive apprenticeship methods try to enculturate students into authentic practices through activity and social interaction in a way similar to that evident—and evidently successful—in craft apprenticeship" (Brown, Collins, and Duguid, 1989, p. 37). Resnick (1987) prefers the term *bridging apprenticeships* to simulate the actual conditions of cognition. Schön (1987) has described the reflective practicum as a way of getting at the tacit knowledge embedded in professional practice. Farmer (1991), focusing on the nature of ill-defined professional problems, argues for a situated approach to resolving practice dilemmas. *Anchored instruction* is another term used (Cognition and Technology Group at Vanderbilt, 1990). Succinctly, Carr (1992, p. 31), in describing the situated relation between cultural institutions and cognition, has said that "learning has to happen with tools literally in hand." Central to all of these notions is the importance of locating cognition in authentic activities through an apprenticeship approach that situates learning in its inherently social, tool-dependent, and interactive context (Brown, Collins, and Duguid, 1989).

From an instructional perspective, this view argues forcibly for removing education from schools and into real situations (indeed, much of the argument for this point of view charges traditional schooling with being demonstrably incapable of providing the learning necessary for human activity in the real world; see Resnick, 1987; Brown, Collins, and Duguid, 1989; Lave, 1988). Rather than present "knowledge" in traditional pedagogic fashion whereby students acquire it, the situated view proposes modeling, coaching, and practice approaches to learning (Cognition and Technology Group at Vanderbilt, 1990; Farmer, 1991; Schön, 1987).

Numerous examples and models of this approach exist. Practicing physicians will claim that it is in their internships and residencies that they first begin to acquire the situated experience and cultural knowledge on which they increasingly build their practice. Similarly, in law it is in case study and clerking that attorneys learn actual law practice. Architects, too, require apprenticeship; from the earliest days of training, architects practice in the same manner that they will use throughout their careers by building models and doing presentations of their plans, which is situationally located, tool dependent, and socially interactive. Likewise, in higher education as well as in the natural and social sciences, research practitioners are required to attend numerous research and methods courses, yet it is in their apprenticeships to senior researchers that the complicated knowing and doing required to solve real research problems is actually gained. Moreover, the importance of apprenticeship is not just evident for white-collar professions. Indeed, this situated framework easily dates back to medieval guild associations. Many occupational groups such as plumbers, electricians, and carpenters require apprenticeships not just to control access to work but also because the knowledge and skill necessary for practice cannot be gained in the classroom. Thus, the argument is that, instructionally, apprenticeship formats allow learners to enter the virtual world of activity (Schön, 1987) where "they must recognize and resolve the ill-defined problems that arise out of authentic activity, in contrast to the well-defined exercises that are typically given to them in text books and on exams throughout their earlier schooling" (Brown, Collins, and Duguid, 1987, p. 40; see also Schön, 1983, 1987).

The implications for adult education could be profound. If the assumptions regarding knowledge and learning transfer are questioned and if the significance of situation is given prominence, then our practice as educators must surely change. Once located in their naturally occurring settings, knowing and learning become intricately integrated with the tools, social interaction, and activity of their use. It is there that we must concentrate our energies and insights as educators by sorting out what is truly transferable from what is situationally specific. It is in this way that cognition will become stretched across mind, body, and culturally organized settings (Lave, 1988). Situated cognition promises to provide a much sounder footing for our education efforts by giving face and form to the long-standing adult education tradition of locating learning in experience.

References

Brown, J. S., Collins, A., and Duguid, P. "Situated Cognition and the Culture of Learning." *Educational Researcher,* 1989, *18* (1), 32–42.
Carr, D. "Cultural Institutions as Structures for Cognitive Change." In L. A. Cavaliere and A. Sgroi (eds.), *Learning for Personal Development.* New Directions for Adult and Continuing Education, no. 53. San Francisco: Jossey-Bass, 1992.
Cognition and Technology Group at Vanderbilt. "Anchored Instruction and Its Relationship to Situated Cognition." *Educational Researcher,* 1990, *19* (6), 2–10.
Dewey, J. *Experience and Education.* New York: Collier, 1938.
Farmer, J. "Helping Adults Learn What They Need to Learn but Cannot Learn Adequately on Their Own." In *Proceedings of the Project for the Study of Adult Learning.* Normal: College of Continuing Education and Public Service, Illinois State University, 1991.
Jarvis, P. *Adult Learning in the Social Context.* London: Croom-Helm, 1987.
Knowles, M. S. *The Modern Practice of Adult Education: From Pedagogy to Andragogy.* (2nd ed.) New York: Cambridge Books, 1980.
Kolb, D. A. *Experiential Learning.* Englewood Cliffs, N.J.: Prentice Hall, 1984.
Lave, J. *Cognition in Practice: Mind, Mathematics and Culture in Everyday Life.* Cambridge, England: Cambridge University Press, 1988.
Lave, J., Murtaugh, M., and de la Rocha, O. "The Dialectic of Arithmetic in Grocery Shopping." In B. Rogoff and J. Lave (eds.), *Everyday Cognition: Its Development in Social Context.* Cambridge, Mass.: Harvard University Press, 1984.
Lindeman, E. *The Meaning of Adult Education.* New York: New Republic, 1926.
Pennington, F., and Green, J. "Comparative Analysis of Program Development in Six Professions." *Adult Education,* 1976, *28,* 13–23.
Resnick, L. B. "Learning in School and Out." *Educational Researcher,* 1987, *16* (9), 13–20.
Rogoff, B. "Introduction." In B. Rogoff and J. Lave (eds.), *Everyday Cognition: Its Development in Social Context.* Cambridge, Mass.: Harvard University Press, 1984.
Rogoff, B., and Lave, J. (eds.). *Everyday Cognition: Its Development in Social Context.* Cambridge, Mass.: Harvard University Press, 1984.
Rubenson, K. "Sociology of Adult Education." In S. B. Merriam and P. M. Cunningham (eds.), *Handbook of Adult and Continuing Education.* San Francisco: Jossey-Bass, 1989.
Schön, D. A. *The Reflective Practitioner: How Professionals Think in Action.* New York: Basic Books, 1983.
Schön, D. A. *Educating the Reflective Practitioner: Toward a New Design for Teaching and Learning in the Professions.* San Francisco: Jossey-Bass, 1987.
Wertsch, J. V. *Vygotsky and the Social Formation of Mind.* Cambridge, Mass.: Harvard University Press, 1985.

ARTHUR L. WILSON *is assistant professor of adult and community education in the Department of Educational Leadership, Ball State University, Muncie, Indiana.*

Jürgen Habermas's works help us to think imaginatively about knowledge, learning, and the human condition. Many adult educators draw on his ideas to provide them with an ideal standard for their education practice and a deep understanding of the cardinal purpose of the adult education vocation.

The Contribution of Critical Theory to Our Understanding of Adult Learning

Michael R. Welton

At first glance, Jürgen Habermas seems an unlikely candidate for attention from the American adult education community. Born in Dusseldorf, Germany, in 1929, Habermas came of age in National Socialist Germany. During his formative years, Habermas experienced the irrationality and barbarism of Nazism. How was it conceivable that Germany, the home of great apostles of enlightenment such as Luther, Kant, Hegel, and Marx, could descend into gas chambers and torchlight parades? Was it really possible to create a rational society after Auschwitz? How was it possible for a scientifically literate and technologically sophisticated society to place its knowledge and technique in the service of evil? Was it possible for human beings to free themselves from irrational ways of ordering their common life? These questions, originating in Habermas's childhood and teenage years, have been central to his writings over the last three decades.

In this chapter, I examine Habermas's ideas about human knowing, language, and social evolution. I argue that Habermas provides us with a fresh way of looking at adult learning in social and historical contexts. This is his major strength. But I also argue that Habermasian insights hold promise for our education practice.

Knowledge, Learning, and the Human Condition

Critical theory is often identified with a talented group of German thinkers who were associated with the Institute of Social Research in Frankfurt

(Theodor Adorno, Max Horkheimer, Herbert Marcuse, and Walter Benjamin). These men believed that life had to be transformed. When they began writing in the early 1920s, they had to make sense of the carnage of battlefields such as the Somme and to grasp the meaning of the Russian Revolution. As the 1920s unfolded into the global depression of the 1930s, they tried to understand the rise of fascism, the collapse of liberal democracy, the growth of new forms of production, and the birth of mass culture. In the 1920s, influenced by Marx's writings, they still believed that the industrial working class was the group that would bring about a more just and free society. By the outbreak of World War II, these Frankfurt thinkers had abandoned several fundamental Marxian axioms. They no longer believed that the industrial working class (the "proletariat") would usher in a better world.

Habermas is a critical theorist of the second generation. He agreed with his Frankfurt teachers that Marxism had to be updated for a new time. He did not accept the brooding pessimism of his mentors. Habermas set out on a very ambitious journey. He wanted to travel back to Marx to find out where he went wrong and then travel forward to his own time to scout the intellectual scene for ideas to make sense of the changed world of post–World War II Europe and America. He appreciated Marx's bold and scholarly attempt to explain why nineteenth-century industrial capitalism produced simultaneously abundant wealth and mammoth misery. But he thought that Marx was wrong to believe that he was writing a "science" of society. Habermas believed that Marx had overestimated the place of science in human life. But what was the proper role of natural scientific knowing in our world? And how could a theory purporting to explain and change the world be justified?

Habermas believed that the natural scientific way of knowing is not the only valid kind of knowledge. In his celebrated and controversial *Knowledge and Human Interests,* Habermas (1972) offered a way of thinking about human knowledge and learning that eventually captured the imagination of many adult education thinkers. From its inception as a university-based field, the study of adult education has been plagued by the (almost) intractable problem of how to define the boundaries of the field. Theorists and practitioners have been struck by the diversity of adult education practices and have almost despaired of finding any underlying unity in the diversity. Habermas developed a way of thinking about the relationship between knowledge, learning, and the human condition that provided a powerful means of understanding the unity in the diversity of human learning processes and outcomes.

Habermas contended that knowledge can take three different forms: technical, practical, and emancipatory. All societies exist in a material environment and must interact with nature to produce their existence. Habermas named this learning domain "labor." Humankind's interchange with nature generates a *technical* interest in prediction and control. All societies, from tribal to modern, learn along the axis of interaction with nature. Only in modern societies is learning about nature expressed in the natural scientific form known as positivism. But all societies also involve "symbolic interaction," the communication of persons with one another. Human interchange creates a *practical* interest in the understanding of meaning. Contemporary social sciences and humanities (anthropology, sociology, literary criticism, history) are called hermeneutical sciences (hermeneutics is the science of interpretation) because they study how human beings make meaning and reach consensus. Finally, every society manifests various forms of power relations among members. *Emancipatory* knowledge derives from humankind's desire to achieve emancipation from domination, whether domination of nature over human life or the domination of some individuals or groups over others. For Habermas, then, knowledge is the outcome of human activity motivated by interests that guide and shape their learning processes.

Human beings learn through the generation of application of technical knowledge (there is cumulative growth in technical and scientific knowledge) and through the generation and application of practical and moral knowledge (there are changes over time in our beliefs, values, and rules governing our interactions). The emancipatory interest is derivative of the others and the most significant. The forms of knowledge guided by the technical and practical interests are always open to questioning and reexamination. But reason also demands explicitly nondistorted communication. A critical social science cannot rest satisfied with discovering regularities in our social action. It must also ask whether our beliefs, values, and interactions express dominative relations that can, in principle, be changed. Each learning domain has its own logic and cannot be reduced to any other (Giddens, 1985; Bernstein, 1985; Held, 1980).

Habermas's theory of knowledge-constitutive interests has captured the imagination of many adult educators and social thinkers. The idea that not all learning can be pressed into a single mold spoke to educators living and working in a world in which technical control over things and people seemed all-pervasive. A philosophy of adult learning influenced by Habermas starts with the affirmation that human beings are *material* and *historical* beings who have the potential to learn about nature, others, and the self. This learning is cumulative through time and is embodied in our ideologies, institutions, and social practices. It is also true, claims Habermas, that human learning can be blocked and distorted. In sum, human beings have the capacity to become active, reflective creatures. But the conditions of our lives (the institutions and values that shape us) often prevent us from acquiring the competencies needed to develop and unfold our many-sided potentialities. The clearest articulation of this philosophy of adult learning is in Fay's (1987) *Critical Social Science: The Limits to Liberation*. This framework is also implicit in Michael Collins's (1991) *Adult Education as Vocation* and my book, *Toward Development Work* (Welton, 1991).

The work of Jack Mezirow illustrates a second way in which adult educators have incorporated Habermasian ideas about the different forms of human knowledge. He analyzes Habermas's work to help him think about the fundamental purpose of the adult educator. Mezirow deserves considerable credit for introducing Habermasian ideas to a field known for its pragmatism. In his writings over almost two decades, Mezirow has been arguing that the cardinal purpose of the educator of adults is to foster critical reflection, namely, to help learners "become critically aware of the cultural and psychological assumptions that have influenced the way we see ourselves and our relationships and the way we pattern our lives" (Mezirow, 1978, p. 101). Mezirow believes that Habermas has established beyond reasonable doubt the existence of three distinct learning domains, each governed by a particular knowledge interest. Each "learning domain suggests . . . a different mode of personal learning and different learning needs" (Mezirow, 1981, p. 143). In *Transformative Dimensions of Adult Learning,* Mezirow (1991) draws on a wide range of sources to make his case. He thinks that the emancipatory interest of human beings is of cardinal significance because our critical reflection on learning blockages has the potential to change the way in which we as human beings communicate with others and nature.

Habermas's reflection on learning domains opens up previously closed lines of questioning. Should adult educators go along with corporate-defined agendas for the training of workers? Should we accept the restricted ways in which competence is defined by some educators and policymakers? Habermasian-influenced adult educators think of worker education as the process of becoming knowledgeable about the way in which the structure of work enables or impedes human development and learning, including acquiring the ability to participate freely in communication processes within the enterprise and learning to be skillful in executing technically appropriate job tasks (Marsick, 1987; Hart, 1992).

Importance of Language

Habermas's (1984, 1987) theory of communicative action is based on the idea that all human communication involves validity claims, and that an ideal speech situation is presupposed every time we use language. According to Habermas, when one person says something to another, that person makes the following claims (implicitly and sometimes explicitly): (1) What is said is comprehensible, that is, it obeys certain rules of language so that there is a meaning that can be understood by the other. (2) The propositional content (the factual assertions) of whatever is said is true.

(3) The speaker is justified in saying whatever is said. In other words, when we use speech in any given context, we invoke certain social rights or "norms." And (4) the speaker is sincere in whatever is said, that is, he or she does not intend to deceive the listener.

To illustrate Habermas's abstract concept of an ideal speech situation, let us suppose that in response to a traveler's question a ticket clerk at a railway station says, "That will be $25 for a cheap day return." The passenger might not initially know what the phrase "cheap day return" means. When the clerk explains what the phrase means, he or she is justifying the first claim. It is implicit in what the clerk says that factual content of the statement is true: It actually does cost $25 for the ticket (the second validity claim). It is also likely that the passenger will take for granted that it is appropriate for the clerk to pronounce authoritatively about the price of the ticket (the third validity claim). And it is also assumed that the clerk sincerely believes what he or she says (the fourth validity claim; see Giddens, 1985, pp. 128–129).

Habermas argues that these four validity criteria serve as a measuring stick for every interaction. They are implicit in all communication, but we become especially aware of them when we are forced, during a conflict, to justify our arguments. In every interaction (face-to-face, organizational, and political-economic policy-making levels), a speaker may speak more or less comprehensibly, sincerely, appropriately, and truthfully. Each of the four criteria allows us to see when interpersonal agreement has been distorted, and how different types of misinformation influence participation in face-to-face and collective decision making.

The first criterion, comprehensibility, requires that people reveal what they mean to one another. Adult learners cannot learn about themselves and others when speech is ambiguous, confused, or nonsensical. At the organizational level, for instance, jargon may be used to exclude others from understanding important matters. The second criterion, sincerity, demands that listeners check the speaker's intentions. The communicative learning process is ruptured when listeners cannot trust the speaker and believe that, despite rhetorical reassurances, the real motive of the speaker has been disguised. Critically reflective learning exposes unexpressed interests (for example, an instrumental or strategic interest in controlling the agenda to maximize control over select resources).

The third criterion, appropriateness or legitimacy, asks, "Is this right?" Here, the concern is with determining proper roles and contexts. How responsive is the speaker to the views of others? Are professionals dominating the discourse? Critically reflective learning positions one to say, "I don't need to accept that," and to ask if decisions are being made in a participatory manner. The final criterion, truth, is guided by the checking of evidence. The question "Is this true?" directs attention to whether information is withheld, responsibility obscured, or need misrepresented. To what extent are decisions being made on insufficient or inadequately interpreted data? Is the learning process democratized or collaborative?

Imagine a community meeting in a rural township. Adult educators have been working for months with local communities to help them understand the impact of a proposed waste disposal site on the ecosystem and to explore alternatives. At the meeting, politicians, businesspeople, environmentalists, and local people are scheduled to speak. From the outset, community members do not trust the politicians and businesspeople to speak sincerely or truthfully. As these individuals speak, community members soon realize that the fourth validity criterion, truthfulness, has not been met. The politicians have not mentioned an authoritative environmental impact study that pointed to the serious threat to the fragile ecosystem if the waste disposal site is approved. The business views are questioned because they are perceived to reflect narrow interests. And the community members are also very angry that the learning process regarding waste disposal was not open and collaborative. Indeed, the adult educators had to fight each step of the way to be allowed to even see background documents.

Each of these criteria—comprehensibility, sincerity, legitimacy, and truthfulness—helps the adult educator to identify the particular competencies required of learners to demystify distorted speech, expose unexpressed interests, and democratize their common life. The concept of an ideal speech situation enables us to compare reality with a fixed standard and to assess the extent to which our modern institutions approximate the ideal.

Habermas is not advocating an ideal form of life in which violence, manipulation, and conflict disappear. Indeed, he believes that "relations of force" are often "inconspicuously set" in the "very structures of communication" and prevent humans from mutual understanding (Habermas, 1979, pp. 119–120). Habermas encourages us to overcome the obstacles that inhibit undistorted and noncoercive communication. For adult educators, this means the cultivation of pedagogical practices that enable all learners to enter into a communicative relationship obligated to make their utterances intelligible, to provide good grounds for their assertions, and to justify their values in a sincere way. Fundamentally, Habermasian-influenced adult educators attempt to create rule-structured communication conditions that enable free and noncoercive learning to occur.

Society and Personal Worlds

Habermas, like his Frankfurt teachers, is profoundly aware of the dark side of our modern technological societies. The evidence is everywhere: the degradation of ecosystems, the reduction of politics to the administration of things, the triumph of instrumental rationality, and the spiritual aridity of mass consumerism. The iron cage and not the promised land of universal freedom appears to have greeted us down modernity's bewitching road. But Habermas does not share his mentors' perception that modern history is one long nightmare. He thinks that modern societies manifest both potential and pathology.

Living in the modern world demands that we give valid reasons for our thinking and action. By so doing, we are shaken free from taken-for-granted ways of seeing and acting. We cannot simply depend on someone else's view of truth, goodness, or beauty. Modernity pushes us all toward being active and reflective persons. But the process of becoming an autonomous, reflective person is not an easy pathway. In our modern age, we are attempting to steer our way through a world of great risk and anxiety. The modern self is threatened by feelings of powerlessness, meaninglessness, and uncertainty. But, Habermas insists, we cannot return to the cocoon of traditional, dogmatic societies. We must learn to see the new possibilities of personal and social learning about meaning that are opening up before us.

Habermas uses the concepts of system and lifeworld to understand how much communicative rationality exists in the modern world. For Habermas, the system has to do with the economy, coded as money, and the state administrative system, coded as power (which he calls the state and corporate steering apparatuses). Systems are defined as organizations of purely strategic actions; that is, people in command positions in systems use a form of reason that represses human norms or values. The objects of corporate and state administrative decisions are acted on from the outside in a way that is inaccessible to reflection. Habermas claims that the capitalist economic system, the legal-rational political system, and even the modern mass communications system employ media such as money and power in a largely coercive, anticommunicative way.

For Habermas, the lifeworld is where "everyday practice" and "everyday communication" occur. The lifeworld is communicatively shared. In our families, places of worship, and schools, we acquire a background of shared meanings. This background of shared meanings makes ordinary symbolic interaction possible. It also provides the background for the legitimation of society and patterns of self-formation. It is in the lifeworld that we come to understand our ethical obligations to family, friends, and society. Adequate socialization processes require competent reference persons to help individuals to become communicatively competent actors.

Habermas does not think that the lifeworld and system world act on each other to mutual benefit. He uses the metaphor "colonization of the lifeworld" to show how the system has become uncoupled from communicatively shared experience and is now steered by the media of money and power. The uncoupling metaphor, however, should not be interpreted to mean that the economic and state administrative systems are detached totally from the lifeworld. The lifeworld always remains related to or embedded in the system. But the lifeworld is now subjected to incessant pressure from the economy and the state. Family and daily work life are pressed into the service of the imperatives of an instrumental rationality. Human beings as childrearers, partners, workers, clients, citizens, and consumers struggle against the process of being turned into objects of corporate and state management. Systemic imperatives, then, threaten to disempower men and women who have the capacity to be empowered, reflective actors.

Collins argues that a "thoughtful pedagogy" must be committed to sustaining lifeworld interests. Like Habermas, Collins is alarmed at the extent of the erosion of skills within lifeworld contexts. Professional experts have colonized areas that "formerly belonged to the everyday lifeworld of reasonably competent, attentive adults" (Collins, 1991, p. 94). Here one thinks of health care, home economics, and community-based services. For example, consider the way in which professional medical experts have, over time, rendered so many of us dependent on their knowledge and services. As we have become more dependent, we have been blocked from learning to be knowledgeable about our mental and physical health. Many of us can scarcely identify where the spleen is located! In the area of home economics, our dependence on prepackaged foods has robbed us of knowledge about food, its nutrients, preparation, and meaning. We no longer have much sense of the relationship between our health and well-being and the foods that we eat. Many other examples could be given.

A thoughtful and enlightened pedagogy would, therefore, be impelled by a vision of a lifeworld and system world acting on each other to mutual benefit. Adult educators would work within industrial and bureaucratic organizations, steered by an ideology of technique, to create democratic learning communities. Adult educators would also support community-based initiatives, such as antinuclear and other new social movement actions, to "protect life-world interests" (Collins, 1991, p. 97). Adult educators who agree with Habermas's indictment of modern technological society must help adult learners acquire the requisite competencies to engage in free and noncoerced dialogue and to work with others to recreate institutions, large and small, that do not "nullify . . . genuine democratic discourse" (Collins, 1991, p. 112).

Conclusion

In this chapter, I have tried to sketch Habermas's main ideas and point to their significance for North American adult educators. Habermas is a very complex thinker, and the academic discussions of his work are very intricate, sometimes ambiguous, and often difficult to grasp. Nonetheless, his thought opens up new and interesting ways of thinking about adult learning in historical and social contexts.

First, the idea that there are three distinct types of knowledge—technical, practical, and emancipatory—offers the North American adult education community one promising way of building an adequate philosophical framework for our field of study and, in particular, for our understanding of adult learning and the nature of knowledge. Second, Habermas's theory of communicative action provides adult educators who are committed to an emancipatory education practice with an ideal standard for their pedagogical work. He challenges adult educators to consider why we have been blind to the ways in which institutions enable or constrain our capacity to learn to be the kind of persons we most want to be. Third, Habermas helps us think about how adult educators can assist in creating developmental, learner-centered, and emancipatory institutions within which individuals can find purpose and identity and become "active, innovative, responsible, and thus happy persons" (Bellah and others, 1991, p. 50). Habermas believes that while all institutions are educative, not all are true learning communities. An institution, whether family, corporation, or state agency, may be organized to block free and noncoerced learning processes. Habermas encourages us to ask whether our institutions, large and small, truly enable human beings to unfold their potentials (cognitive, moral, technical, aesthetic) in their daily routine interactions. Fourth, Habermas provides adult educators with a language to think about the pathologies and potentialities of modern technological societies. He encourages us to understand that technical rationality is only one valid way of knowing, and that our technological knowledge about how to "master" nature ought to be in the service of our moral vision of a developmentally humanist society (one that distributes learning chances equitably throughout the society). Fifth, Habermas's ideas about the interplay of system and lifeworld help us to understand the adult educator's vocation. Collins's idea of a "thoughtful pedagogy" committed to sustaining lifeworld interests represents an important way of formulating the central purpose of the North American adult educator.

References

Bellah, R. N., and others. *The Good Society.* New York: Knopf, 1991.

Bernstein, R. "Introduction." In R. Bernstein (ed.), *Habermas and Modernity.* London: Polity Press, 1985.

Collins, M. *Adult Education as Vocation.* New York: Routledge & Kegan Paul, 1991.

Fay, B. *Critical Social Science: The Limits to Liberation.* Ithaca, N.Y.: Cornell University Press, 1987.

Giddens, A. "Jürgen Habermas." In Q. Skinner (ed.), *The Return of Grand Theory in the Human Sciences.* New York: Cambridge University Press, 1985.

Habermas, J. *Knowledge and Human Interests.* Portsmouth, N.H.: Heinemann Educational Books, 1972.

Habermas, J. *Communication and the Evolution of Society.* Boston: Beacon Press, 1979.

Habermas, J. *Theory of Communicative Action.* Vol. 1. Boston: Beacon Press, 1984.

Habermas, J. *Theory of Communicative Action.* Vol. 2. Boston: Beacon Press, 1987.

Hart, M. *Working and Educating for Life: Feminist and International Perspectives on Adult Education.* New York: Routledge & Kegan Paul, 1992.

Held, D. *Introduction to Critical Theory: Horkheimer to Habermas.* London: Hutchinson, 1980.

Marsick, V. (ed.). *Learning in the Workplace.* London: Croom-Helm, 1987.

Mezirow, J. D. "Perspective Transformation." *Adult Education,* 1978, 28 (2).

Mezirow, J. D. "A Critical Theory of Adult Learning and Education." *Adult Education Quarterly,* 1981, 32 (1), 3–27.

Mezirow, J. *Transformative Dimensions of Adult Learning.* San Francisco: Jossey-Bass, 1991.

Welton, M. R. *Toward Development Work.* Geelong, South Victoria, Australia: Deakin University Press, 1991.

MICHAEL R. WELTON *is associate professor of adult education at Dalhousie University, Halifax, Nova Scotia. He is interested in the foundations of adult education and has published widely on historical and critical theoretical topics.*

The feminist pedagogy literature is beginning to have an impact on the field of adult education and offers new strategies for challenging power relations based on gender, race, and class in the adult learning environment.

Feminism and Adult Learning: Power, Pedagogy, and Praxis

Elizabeth J. Tisdell

We were in an adult learning class. There were eighteen students in the class, thirteen women and five men. I was a student in the class, and our task on that night was to break into four small groups to discuss and then present or act out a particular theory of adult learning. Members of my group had done their homework well; we had a good handle on Bandura's social learning theory, the theory that we were to present, so we busily began planning our presentation. We decided that Paul, the only male student in our group, would be the narrator while the rest of us would act out what he, as narrator, explained. As each group made their presentations, we were entertained and amazed by both the creativity of our peers and what we had learned in the process about adult learning theory. But when all was said and done, the not-so-readily apparent dynamics were, to me, far more fascinating. Even though there were two to three times as many women as men in the class and in each group, every group had done what my group had: chosen a male student for the lead role in the presentation.

It was not that each group consciously decided that the person in the lead role should be male. After all, such choices are usually made unconsciously, and often it does not matter how "politically correct" or intellectually sophisticated one's rational thinking is about gender, race, or class issues. In fact, in the scenario described above, I was the one who suggested quite offhandedly that Paul be the narrator. I was not thinking that we needed a male leader, nor was I even thinking about the fact that Paul was male. Rather, I was intent on the task at hand—how to put our skit together to portray Bandura's social learning theory. One might think that this is an isolated instance. After all, somebody had to be in the lead role, and it just happened to be Paul this time. True enough, but when all four groups also chose a male for the lead role, especially when the number of males was so limited in this class, it seemed that there was something more going on than met the eye.

Situations like these are not merely coincidental. It is no secret that males (and others who benefit from systems of privilege in our culture, such as those who are white, middle-class, or able-bodied) are often chosen for leadership positions over females (or racial minorities, members of the working class, or people with disabilities) in the professional world of work. But they are also more often in leadership roles, either overtly or covertly, in less formal situations, such as in voluntary organizations, in social gatherings, and, as we have seen in the above vignette, in the adult education classroom. It is not necessarily that these males consciously "take over" the groups in which they participate, or that women (or members of those less privileged populations cited above) consciously acquiesce or set the males up to be in leadership positions instead of themselves.

This process of putting (mostly white) men in either informal or formal leadership positions is instead more unconscious in nature. It is probably a result of the fact that we are, after all, accustomed to having men in leadership positions in all places in our society. The adult education classroom is no exception. Men, especially white men, have been socialized to be in leadership roles. Not only do they often willingly volunteer for such roles, but they also have been socialized to speak with a more authoritative style than women, which makes them more likely to be chosen for such roles. Women, on the other hand, have been socialized to be in support roles, to defer to men, and to take care of people, sometimes at their own expense. They may contribute to the process of putting men in leadership roles by suggesting a particular man for one of those roles, especially if they perceive that he wants to be in that role, in order to take care of him. Or women can simply refuse to volunteer for a variety of reasons. No matter what the reasons are, the reality is clear: In general, males and those who benefit from greater privilege in our society because of their race, class, age, or experience have more power than do women, racial minorities, and members of the working class in the adult education classroom. The question is, What can be or is being done about it?

The role of adult education in changing the nature of unequal power relations between privileged and oppressed groups is a concern expressed in the adult education literature (for example, Collard and Law, 1989; Cunningham, 1988; Freire, 1971). Cunningham (1988) has argued that adult educators have an ethical responsibility to create environments where people can come to an understanding of how the realities of their lives were created. This means helping people explore what the nature of structured power relations has to do with the realities of their personal lives. For example, what does being born black, or being born into a working-class family, or being female from a particular religious tradition mean in regard to how much opportunity, power, or control one has in one's family, workplace, and personal life? And what are the spoken and unspoken rules regarding how an individual from one such background is supposed to act in groups (including classroom groups) with people who have different status? The creation of an environment where students can examine the connection between their personal situations and the structured power relations between privileged and oppressed groups in our society leads to a more conscious and informed understanding of their lives and may contribute to their emancipation.

The question of how best to educate for social transformation has no easy answer. It has long been an issue for adult educators interested in emancipatory education. The recent feminist pedagogy literature offers new insights that may prove useful for adult education practitioners who try to educate for social transformation. In order to outline how feminist theory and feminist pedagogy can offer new insights both to the field of adult learning and to those educators interested in educating for social transformation, the following discussion has three parts. First, an explanation of feminist pedagogy and an examination of its underlying assumptions are provided. Second, how feminist theory and pedagogy offer new insights for an understanding of learning in adulthood is considered. Finally, the impact of feminist pedagogy literature on the field and the implications of incorporating feminist theory and pedagogy in the practice of adult education are discussed.

What Is Feminist Pedagogy?

A wide body of literature reflects the orientation known as feminist pedagogy. While the various strands of feminist pedagogy have been influenced by different educational models, all strands share a concern with the following issues: (1) how to teach women more effectively so that they gain a sense of their ability to effect change in their own lives, (2) an emphasis on connection and relationship (rather than separation) with both the knowledge learned and the facilitator and other learners, and (3) women's emerging sense of personal power. All of the feminist pedagogy literature is emancipatory in the broad sense in that it is concerned with women's personal empowerment (Hayes, 1989; Maher, 1987).

However, it is important to point out that not all of the feminist pedagogy literature deals with the nature of structured power relationships or with women's collective experience as an oppressed group. The strand of the feminist pedagogy literature that stops short of dealing with structured power relations deals only with women's personal empowerment from a developmental-psychological perspective. Maher (1987) has suggested that the wide body of literature coming to be labeled feminist pedagogy can be divided into two major subgroups that have been influenced by two major educational models. She called these two models the "liberatory" model and the "gender" model and examined the strengths and weaknesses of each. The philosophical assumptions of each of the models are examined below.

Liberatory Model. The liberatory or emancipatory model of feminist pedagogy deals with the nature of structured power relations and interlocking systems of oppression based on gender, race, class, age, and so on. In particular, versions of the liberatory model attempt to account for and deal with why it is that women (and minorities) are often silenced or absent or that their contributions are overlooked or discounted in the public arenas of our society, including government, industry, education, and in the classroom at all education levels. These models of feminist pedagogy have critical theory and the work of the neo-Marxist education theorists, along with feminist reinterpretations of those theories, at their root. Feminist education theorists who write from the perspective of the liberatory model have been heavily influenced by Freire's (1971) work, but they have also been critical of Freire and Marxist education theories because their primary focus has been on class-based oppression. Freire and his followers have not dealt adequately with oppression based on gender, race, or interlocking systems of oppression such as gender and race, or gender and class, or gender, race, and class.

Most feminist emancipatory education theorists operating from the liberatory perspective are influenced by a socialist-feminist or feminist-materialist theoretical understanding of society and its power relations. The underlying philosophical assumption of feminist materialism is that the material realities of people's lives—the physical realities of maleness or femaleness, race, material needs for food and shelter, and so on—shape or affect all other aspects of people's sociocultural lives, including their values (Chafetz, 1988).

Consider education as a sociocultural value. There is likely to be a difference in the value that a white middle-class male versus a black working-class woman with two children place on education because of the difference in the material realities that inform each of their lives. Consider the experience of both of them when in an educational situation. In order to even be able to take part in that educational activity, the black working-class woman is much more likely than the male to need someone to take care of her children. Once child care is arranged and she is present for the educational experience, she and the white middle-class male are likely to have very different experiences in the situation. The white middle-class male will probably feel much more validated by the experience. After all, most of the so-called experts in any field of study are likely to be white middle-class males, and most of the examples used in the books and curriculum materials are probably about people who are also white and middle class. Society at large has been taught to value what people that look, think, and talk like him have to say. But for the black woman, neither "the experts" nor most of the examples used in the books are about people that look, think, or talk like her. Moreover, she has probably been taught that her speech pattern is "incorrect," and she has to learn to write and speak in a style that some other group has determined is "correct"; therefore, the society is not predisposed to pay that much attention to what she has to say. In addition, because of her working-class status, she also has less money to spend on education or educational supports such as child care, transportation, tutors, and books. If she succeeds in spite of all of these obstacles, it is likely that she will be paid less than her white male counterpart in the workplace for the same job. Thus, it is easy to understand why she might value formal education less than the white middle-class male. It has different returns for her because of the material realities of her life—her different gender, her different race, and her different class background.

For some of the reasons noted in the above example, many feminist emancipatory education theorists suggest that the oppression of women in both the paid work force and the domestic labor realm is *reproduced* by events in the classroom. Because the curriculum, the knowledge base, and the examples used in the books and materials are created by and are primarily about the white middle-class male experience, white middle-class males are more likely to be successful both in the education system and in a society that accords greater value to that experience. Therefore, white male privilege is reproduced by the system. Because the experience of women of all races is either absent or is presented in the curriculum in a way that reinforces their subservience, they are taught in both overt and covert ways to be subservient in the education system as well as in society. Thus, the oppression of women in general is reproduced. This is true for race and class relations as well (Weiler, 1988).

Reproduction theory accounts for how power relations in society are partially reproduced by the education system. It does not, however, account for the fact that a number of women and members of minority and working-class groups have been as successful as their white male counterparts and have assumed leadership positions both in the education system and in society. For this reason, other feminist education theorists operating from the liberatory model focus more on the forms of resistance that women and minorities adopt in order to create meaning in the education system and in a society that has been designed to help reproduce the existing power relations. Resistance theorists are concerned with how teachers and students *produce* meaning through their own resistance and their own cultural experience.

Feminist resistance theorists discuss the many ways in which women and girls have resisted adoption of the values of the white middle-class culture. In a study examining black and white working-class women's ways of knowing in community-based adult education programs, Luttrell (1989) found that the women of both races resisted placing too much importance on the white middle-class value on knowledge advanced by school authorities. Both the black and white women distinguished between common sense and intelligence. Common sense, a characteristic that both the black and white women attributed to themselves, was defined as the ability to negotiate working-class culture and to solve day-to-day problems. Intelligence was not as clearly defined, but, overall, a distinction was made between school-based intelligence and "real intelligence."

Real intelligence was seen as the ability to teach oneself a skill such as how to fix a car or play a musical instrument. In defining who had real intelligence, the white women gave only male examples. They included the manual labor typical of males, such as the ability to fix mechanical items, in their examples of real intelligence, but the skilled labor required of them as women—the ability to sew, quilt, or cook—was never cited as instances of real intelligence. The black women, on the other hand, saw the work that they did as requiring real intelligence; many also specifically cited the ability to deal with racism and survive as instances of real intelligence. While the black women defined themselves as having real intelligence, they "attribute black men's power to black men's superior knowledge" (Luttrell, 1989, p. 43), saying that black men have the ability to convince black women to do just what the women said they would never do. Thus, even though the black women saw themselves as having real intelligence, black men's intelligence was seen as superior to their own. Both the black and white women resisted adoption of the white middle-class value of the importance of school-based knowledge. But both groups adopted the gender-oppressive value of male intellectual superiority, although in different ways.

In summary, there appear to be three central themes in feminist resistance theory (Weiler, 1988). First, all people have the capacity to be the creators and producers of meaning in their lives and to resist the forces of oppression. Second, the forms that such resistance takes are influenced by multiple factors of oppression, including race, class, gender, age, sexual orientation, and ethnicity. Third, the various forms of resistance that people use, based on the multiple factors of race, class, gender, and so on, may sometimes propagate other forms of oppression or domination of themselves or other people.

Gender Model. The liberatory model of feminist emancipatory education focuses on the structured power relations and interlocking systems of oppression that affect women's lives both in society and in the classroom. The gender model, on the other hand, deals directly with women's socialization as nurturers. The gender model is emancipatory in the personal psychological sense, but it is not emancipatory in terms of dealing with the power relations of the larger social structure.

Belenky, Clinchy, Goldberger, and Tarule's (1986) book, *Women's Ways of Knowing: The Development of Self, Voice, and Mind*, is probably the most often-cited work in contemporary feminist pedagogy operating from the gender model. The authors interviewed a total of 135 women of different races, classes, and ages about the ways in which they best came to know and learn. They found that women learn best in environments that emphasize connected teaching and learning. In these environments, women begin to recognize their own ability to think independently, to think critically, and to come to their own conclusions. It is also in these connected teaching-learning situations that many women come to recognize and hear their own voices.

Connected teachers, as defined by Belenky, Clinchy, Goldberger, and Tarule (1986), see the teacher as midwife. The teacher's task is to draw students out, to "assist the students in giving birth to their own ideas, in making their own tacit knowledge explicit and elaborating on it" (1986, p. 217), and to support the evolution of the students' own thinking. In connected teaching, the student begins to integrate the private and the public, the personal and the political. For example, a woman in an algebra class might finally understand how to calculate percentages when she realizes that she has always been able to figure out how much to leave for a 15 or 20 percent tip in a real-life situation. Or a woman in a psychology class might make the connection between the societal forces that reinforce male privilege when she realizes that most psychological theories have been based on research conducted with white male samples.

It is clear that Belenky, Clinchy, Goldberger, and Tarule (1986) are concerned about the personal empowerment and individual development of the student as well as how that sense of personal power can be developed through overt and hidden aspects of the curriculum. While, ideally, the relationship between the personal and the collective comes to light in the education process, Belenky, Clinchy, Goldberger, and Tarule appear to be primarily concerned with the students' emerging sense of personal power and ability to effect change in their lives. These authors would probably argue that change in one's personal life ultimately effects social change, but they appear to be only secondarily concerned with structural change and political action. Other educators, such as those who operate with the liberatory model discussed earlier, are more concerned with the role of education in structural change, and they more directly deal with power issues not only in society but also in the classroom. As Maher (1987) has suggested, a synthesis of both the liberatory and the gender models may offer new possibilities for teaching and learning.

Feminist Pedagogy and Adult Learning

Based on the above discussion, what insights does the feminist emancipatory education or feminist pedagogy literature offer for learning in adulthood? A synthesis of both the liberatory and the gender models initially offers three primary and interrelated insights for adult learning.

First, it is clear that the feminist emancipatory education literature suggests that women may have different learning needs from men. Nearly all education systems have been initially designed for the education of men, with a knowledge base predominantly based on a rationality that was socially constructed by white males. Belenky, Clinchy, Goldberger, and Tarule (1986) suggest that women seem to do best in learning environments where affective forms of knowledge or knowledge that comes from life experience are valued. In short, they do best in learning environments where there is an effort to relate theoretical concepts to real-life experience.

Clearly, the idea of capitalizing on students' life experiences and relating theoretical concepts to those experiences is not new in the adult education literature. Nevertheless, the feminist pedagogy literature centers on the importance of women in particular reclaiming and validating the learning that comes from their life experience *as women*. Because women have a different relationship to the structures of power from that of men, there has been a tendency to dismiss or discount their learning that comes from experience in the private realm.

Belenky, Clinchy, Goldberger, and Tarule's (1986) connected teaching methods and learning environments seem to help women begin to see themselves as creators of knowledge. The creation of connected learning environments helped at least some women in their study begin to integrate subjective knowledge, where truth is perceived as personal, private, and internally derived, with procedural knowledge, where objective procedures are used for deriving or obtaining knowledge. Women who were able to integrate subjective and procedural forms of knowledge came to see themselves as more independent thinkers, and Belenky, Clinchy, Goldberger, and Tarule report that these women were more concerned with moral and spiritual values and began to translate their moral views and commitments into action. When attempting to solve moral dilemmas and to translate ideas into action, they tended to ask questions related to context. Thus, connected learning environments may help women see themselves as independent thinkers and constructors of knowledge, which is more likely to lead to social action.

Second, implicit in the discussion of the feminist emancipatory education literature is attention to the sociocultural context where power relations based on the interlocking systems of oppression abound. These power relations are always present and clearly affect learning. Power disparities between women or racial minorities and the white male majority are present in both hidden and overt ways in adult education curricula. As Hugo (1989), Collard and Stalker (1991), and Colin and Preciphs (1991) have pointed out, literature that deals with power issues related to women and minorities is often absent in adult education curricula, and the literature that does deal with women and minorities often portrays them only in nonauthoritative roles, which contributes to the reproduction of unequal power relations in society. The feminist emancipatory education literature calls attention to these issues and underscores the importance of directly dealing with these issues in the sociocultural context—through the choice of what to include in the overt curriculum and in attending to what gets taught through the hidden curriculum by the way in which the class or education program is conducted.

Third, the feminist emancipatory education literature contributes to the adult learning literature in the direct discussion of how to deal with power issues in the learning environment that affect the learning process. There is considerable discussion in the feminist pedagogy literature about the power disparity between the teacher and the student, and how professors, as authorities of their own knowledge, should deal with power issues that come up in their classes. Much of the literature deals with concrete examples based on experience. Since this power disparity is a central theme in much of the feminist emancipatory education literature and of interest to adult educators who want to attempt to deal with power issues and alter the nature of structured power relations in the classroom, some brief examples are in order here.

Gardner, Dean, and McKaig (1989) discuss the reality of trying to deal with power issues in a women's studies class. Gardner, the professor of the class, discusses her effort to make a "truly feminist" classroom. She relinquished most of her authority and took on a passive role in the first part of the class because she did not want to exercise power and domination in her classroom. She found, however, that as a result of relinquishing her own authority as teacher, the feminist majority, those who considered themselves "the enlightened," dominated the class, and those students who either had less of a background in feminism or were less sure of their political position felt silenced. "The students used differences in knowledge to create a distinct hierarchy in the classroom with knowledge being a source of power over others" (Gardner, Dean, and McKaig, 1989, p. 65). A similar dynamic emerged when discussing topics of class, where women from working-class backgrounds felt silenced.

These dynamics caused Gardner to rethink her own position on the issue of teacher authority. She reclaimed some of her authority as teacher and encouraged the class members to critique the power dynamics that emerged in the class. This helped the students grapple with the nature of power relations in a concrete situation. Gardner then concluded that, as an instructor, she can use the power of her role as teacher to facilitate the emancipation of women students.

Black feminist theorist Bell Hooks also addresses this issue of teacher authority in the feminist classroom. She acknowledges that there is a power disparity between teachers and students in classrooms and that it needs to be dealt with openly. She suggests, however, that teachers can use their power in ways that enrich students by directly challenging unequal power relations based on gender, race, and class. Hooks's model of feminist pedagogy differs from the model described by Belenky, Clinchy, Goldberger, and Tarule (1986) in that her style is more confrontational.

> It is a model of pedagogy that is based on the assumption that many students will take courses from me who are afraid to assert themselves as critical thinkers, who are afraid to speak (especially students from oppressed and exploited groups). The revolutionary hope that I bring to the classroom is that it will become a space where they can come to voice. Unlike the stereotypical model that suggests women best come to voice in an atmosphere of safety (one in which we are all going to be kind and nurturing), I encourage students to work at coming to voice in an atmosphere where they may be afraid or see themselves at risk [Hooks, 1989, p. 53].

Hooks (1989) argues that teachers need to be proactive in confronting unequal power relations. Thus, she uses the power of her role to directly challenge the unequal power relations of society. Her perspective, as well as that of Gardner, Dean, and McKaig (1989), on how to deal with power issues in higher education classrooms while bearing in mind the sociocultural context of the students and the learning situation, may offer insights to other adult educators on how to do the same in their own learning environments.

Implications for Practice

The feminist pedagogy and feminist theory literature is just beginning to have an impact on the field of adult education. While there is a body of literature that examines the nature of power relations in the adult education field, there is at present a limited literature base that specifically examines power relations based on gender and race. Colin and Preciphs (1991) have discussed the fact that the curricula in most adult education settings still represent the white worldview. Collard and Stalker (1991) and Hugo (1989) have also pointed out that there has generally been a lack of attention to feminist theory, which uses gender as a unit of analysis in theory development in adult education and adult learning. Hugo (1989) has suggested that feminist theory should be used to critique existing theories in adult education and to offer new insights to the field of adult education. The recent critiques by both Hart (1990) and Clark and Wilson (1991) of Mezirow's theory of perspective transformation (Mezirow and Associates, 1990) have been informed by a feminist analysis. Hart (1992) analyzes work and education from a feminist perspective and makes an outstanding contribution to the workplace learning literature. Thus, there is evidence that the feminist theory and feminist pedagogy literature are in fact beginning to have an impact on the field of adult education and on adult learning theory.

But the feminist pedagogy literature is also beginning to have an impact in the practical realm of adult education. As we come to better understand the ways in which women and minorities know and learn, practitioners who want to raise consciousness or challenge power relations in the adult learning environment are beginning to adopt teaching strategies intended to directly challenge structured power relations. What are some of these teaching strategies and what are the practical implications of the feminist pedagogy literature for adult educators who want to engage in emancipatory education practices?

First, adult educators who want to adopt feminist and emancipatory education practices should carefully consider how their curriculum materials for their classes or learning activities serve to challenge the nature of structured power relations based on gender, race, and class. As Wood (1988) has suggested, decisions about what to include in the curriculum are political considerations. When choosing curriculum materials to address issues related to women and racial minorities, one might consider if such materials examine these issues from the perspective of unequal power relations or from the standpoint of gender or racial differences only. Since books related to content areas often do not include chapters dealing with women and minority issues, it may be necessary to include additional books or articles that specifically address gender, race, and class issues related to the course content or learning opportunity.

Second, adult education instructors who want to challenge structured power relations based on gender, race, and class need to adopt teaching strategies that contribute to the achievement of this goal. Instructors must develop and experiment with teaching strategies that prove over time to be emancipatory. As Belenky, Clinchy, Goldberger, and Tarule (1986) found, teaching strategies that unite theory and practice, that value affective forms of knowledge, and that require reflection on how the course content relates to students' life experiences seem to contribute to the ability of women to find voice. Such an approach may also work for minority students. However, the adoption of such an approach does not mean that critical reflection and discussion of highly theoretical material are unnecessary or impossible in a feminist or emancipatory education classroom, or that students in such classrooms are not challenged (Hooks, 1989). Rather, discussion of highly theoretical concepts must be integrated with a consideration of how they relate to the lives of real people, including the students in the class. Such an approach is not only intellectually stimulating, it also makes the educational experience more meaningful and may be more likely to lead to social action.

Third, while the choice of emancipatory teaching strategies is an individual decision, it is worthwhile for all university departments to develop new courses specifically designed to deal directly with power relations based on gender, race, and class. Development of new learning opportunities dealing with these issues is important, but integration of these issues into the existing curriculum and learning activities is also important for all content areas. Adult educators outside academia might also consider the development of programs that deal with power issues related to their own content areas, such as how these issues might be addressed in the workplace.

Finally, adult educators who are interested in challenging unequal power relations based on gender, race, and class may attempt to address the ways in which their own unconscious behavior in the learning environment either challenges or reproduces society's inequitable distribution of power. We have all unconsciously internalized to some degree the values of the dominant culture. In attempting to increase our consciousness about power relations in the classroom, we may want to consider such issues as the gender, race, and class of the majority of characters in our illustrative stories and examples, who are affirmed (by both facilitators and students) as leaders of the class and how, with whom we have more eye contact, and on whom we rely to carry the discussion (Tisdell, 1992). We may want to watch ourselves on videotape or consider inviting a trusted colleague or friend to observe the way in which we conduct a learning session, paying attention to these issues. One cannot change what one is not conscious of, and the reproduction of power relations happens largely through unconscious mechanisms.

In conclusion, the feminist pedagogy literature is in fact beginning to have an impact on the field of adult education. In the coming years, as theorists continue to use feminist theory to critique present theories of adult learning, those theories are likely to be revised. Further research on the adult learning patterns of women and members of minority groups may also lead to the development of new adult learning theories. And as practitioners continue to adopt some of the principles of feminist pedagogy in their own teaching, there may be an increased sensitivity to gender and minority issues among students and practitioners, leading to even greater insights into the nature of feminist pedagogy and the education of women and minorities. Thus, we look to the future with a growing awareness of gender and minority concerns. May this growing awareness help lead to the emancipation of ourselves and our students.

References

Belenky, M. F., Clinchy, B. M., Goldberger, N. R., and Tarule, J. M. *Women's Ways of Knowing: The Development of Self, Voice, and Mind.* New York: Basic Books, 1986.

Chafetz, J. *Feminist Sociology: An Overview of Contemporary Theories.* Itasca, Ill.: Peacock, 1988.

Clark, M. C., and Wilson, A. "Context and Rationality in Mezirow's Theory of Transformational Learning." *Adult Education Quarterly,* 1991, *41* (2), 75–91.

Colin, S., and Preciphs, T. K. "Perceptual Patterns and the Learning Environment: Confronting White Racism." In R. Hiemstra (ed.), *Creating Environments for Effective Adult Learning.* New Directions for Adult and Continuing Education, no. 50. San Francisco: Jossey-Bass, 1991.

Collard, S., and Law, M. "The Limits of Perspective Transformation: A Critique of Mezirow's Theory." *Adult Education Quarterly,* 1989, *39* (2), 99–107.

Collard, S., and Stalker, J. "Women's Trouble: Women, Gender, and the Learning Environment." In R. Hiemstra (ed.), *Creating Environments for Effective Adult Learning.* New Directions for Adult and Continuing Education, no. 50. San Francisco: Jossey-Bass, 1991.

Cunningham, P. "The Adult Educator and Social Responsibility." In R. G. Brockett (ed.), *Ethical Issues in Adult Education.* New York: Teachers College Press, 1988.

Freire, P. *Pedagogy of the Oppressed.* New York: Herder & Herder, 1971.

Gardner, S., Dean, C., and McKaig, D. "Responding to Differences in the Classroom: The Politics of Knowledge, Class, and Sexuality." *Sociology of Education,* 1989, *62,* 64–74.

Hart, M. "Critical Theory and Beyond: An Emancipatory Education and Social Action." *Adult Education Quarterly,* 1990, *40* (3), 125–138.

Hart, M. *Working and Educating for Life: Feminist and International Perspectives on Adult Education.* New York: Routledge & Kegan Paul, 1992.

Hayes, E. R. "Insights from Women's Experience for Teaching and Learning." In E. R. Hayes (ed.)., *Effective Teaching Styles.* New Directions for Adult and Continuing Education, no. 43. San Francisco: Jossey-Bass, 1989.

Hooks, B. *Talking Back: Thinking Feminist, Thinking Black.* Boston: South End Press, 1989.

Hugo, J. "Adult Education and Feminist Theory." In P. M. Cunningham and J. Ohliger (eds.), *Radical Thinking in Adult Education.* Occasional Papers No. 1. Battle Creek, Mich.: Kellogg Foundation, 1989.

Luttrell, W. "Working-Class Women's Ways of Knowing: Effects of Gender, Race, and Class." *Sociology of Education,* 1989, *62,* 33–46.

Maher, F. A. "Toward a Richer Theory of Feminist Pedagogy: A Comparison of 'Liberation' and 'Gender' Models for Teaching and Learning." *Journal of Education,* 1987, *169* (3), 91–100.

Mezirow, J., and Associates. *Fostering Critical Reflection in Adulthood: A Guide to Transformative and Emancipatory Learning.* San Francisco: Jossey-Bass, 1990.

Tisdell, E. J. "Power Relations in Higher Education Classes of Nontraditional-Age Adults: A Comparative Case Study." Unpublished doctoral dissertation, Department of Adult Education, University of Georgia, 1992.

Weiler, K. *Women Teaching for Change.* South Hadley, Mass.: Bergin & Garvey, 1988.

Wood, G. "Democracy and the Curriculum." In L. Beyer and M. Apple (eds.), *The Curriculum: Problems, Politics, and Possibilities.* Albany: State University of New York Press, 1988.

ELIZABETH J. TISDELL is coordinator of student services for evening classes at the Georgia Center for Continuing Education, University of Georgia. She also teaches in the Women's Studies Program.

This chapter draws on information in previous chapters to assess where we are now in our efforts to build theory about learning in adulthood.

Taking Stock

Sharan B. Merriam

One of the most powerful motivators for participation in adult learning activities is the need to stay abreast of changes in society that affect one's work and personal life. So too, most adult educators want to be informed of new ideas and changes in the field that might have some bearing on practice. We try to be better practitioners by staying up-to-date in our knowledge of the field, by reflecting on this knowledge, and by thoughtfully incorporating it into our practice. The purpose of this volume has been to provide an update on adult learning theory, an area of key importance to all practitioners in adult education. In this last chapter, I reflect on the contributions that both new approaches and old standbys are making to the knowledge base of adult learning.

In Chapter One, I traced the development of adult learning theory from psychologists interested in learning in general, to adult educators interested in formulating adult-specific models, to the recent infusion of insights and theoretical frameworks from other disciplines and perspectives. There is another way to slice the "pie" of adult learning theory, and that is to see how each of the perspectives presented in Chapters Two through Nine tells us more about the adult learner, the learning process, and the context in which learning takes place. The consideration of adult learning from this tripartite framework was first suggested in *Learning in Adulthood: A Comprehensive Guide* (Merriam and Caffarella, 1991). Each of the perspectives reviewed in the present volume can be seen as emphasizing one or the other of learner, process, or context; considered together, we have a broadened understanding of the complex nature of learning in adulthood.

The Adult Learner

A focus on the adult learner defines an approach to understanding adult learning that is particularly characteristic of North American adult educators. Knowles's andragogy, the best-known theory of adult learning, is based on humanistic assumptions about the adult learner: He or she is characterized by an independent self-concept, has a depth and breadth of prior experience that can be used in learning, has a readiness and orientation to learn related to the roles and responsibilities of adult life, and is internally motivated. In Chapter Two, Pratt illuminates for us the assumptions and philosophical orientation underlying andragogy and points out that this orientation has led to two tensions in practice: whether human agency or social structures has the greater influence and how one negotiates the balance between freedom and authority. Pratt's analysis opens up our thinking about the implications of uncritically adopting the andragogical model to guide our practice.

Research and theory building in self-directed learning is another area that focuses primarily on the individual learner. As Caffarella states in Chapter Three, "The focus of learning is on the individual and self-development, with learners expected to assume primary responsibility for their own learning" (p. 26). Another way in which the self-directed learning literature emphasizes the individual is the effort to determine whether adults are naturally autonomous and self-directed in their learning, whether this characteristic is situational, and whether adults can be taught to be more self-directed. While some attention has been given to the process of learning in this manner, the bulk of the literature on self-directed learning has the individual adult learner as its focus.

The learner is also the focus of the three models of adult learning reviewed by Hiemstra in Chapter Four. Cross's Chain of Response and Characteristics of Adults as Learners models, Knox's proficiency theory of adult learning, and McClusky's theory of margin all begin with the adult learner and his or her characteristics, needs, resources, and so on. While these models have not undergone the same theoretical scrutiny or empirical testing as andragogy or self-directed learning, they do present conceptualizations of aspects of adult learning that have the potential for enhancing our understanding of adult learners. Hiemstra suggests how each can be utilized to extend the theory and research base in this area.

It has been primarily adult educators who have studied adult learning from the starting point of understanding the characteristics and motivations of the *learners*. As mentioned in Chapter One, this concern may be a result of the need of adult educators to distinguish adult learning from child learning. Since adulthood is qualitatively different from childhood, then so too might be the learning that goes on in this period of the life cycle.

The Learning Process

An understanding of what actually transpires when learning occurs has been the focus of much of the research in educational psychology from Thorndike onward. Indeed, psychologists, philosophers, and some educators have opened up new pathways in the study of human learning.

Transformational learning theorists such as Mezirow, Daloz, and Freire focus on the dramatic changes in the learners themselves that can occur when adults engage in a learning transaction. Transformational learning is often linked to development, that is, learning changes us in some way, most often in a positive, growth-enhancing direction. The best documentation of this process comes from Mezirow, who posits that a disorienting dilemma leads us to critically reflect on the assumptions and beliefs that have guided our lives. This reflection process can lead to changes in how we structure the meaning systems through which subsequent experiences are filtered. In Mezirow's view, perspective transformations are the defining characteristic of *adult* learning. It is in fact this focus on the learning process, rather than on learner characteristics, that Clark, in Chapter Five, identifies as transformational learning's major contribution to our understanding of adult learning in general. Mezirow's perspective transformation, in particular, offers the field a well-developed conception of adult learning that has informed both the theory and practice of adult education.

In Chapter Six, Boucouvalas reviews the burgeoning body of literature on levels, states, and structures of consciousness and how this knowledge has been applied to learning. From popular subliminal tapes, to meditation, to biofeedback, to chemically-induced states of consciousness, our understanding of learning is being affected by developments in this arena. Equally promising are efforts to uncover and document the wisdom of ancient and native cultures. Boucouvalas rightly points out that this knowledge base expands the context for understanding adult learning both in theory and in practice.

We are also learning more about the process of learning from those who take the immediate context, the people, and the objects or "tools" within the situation into account when trying to explain the cognitive processes of solving everyday life problems. This approach, loosely labeled "situated cognition," broadens our understanding of adult learning in a way different from those interested in consciousness. Spokespersons for this approach often differentiate between learning that occurs in school from learning that occurs in adult life. School learning situations are artificial, while real-life situations are authentic and meaningful contexts for learning. In Chapter Seven, Wilson makes a strong case for adult educators to approach learning from this perspective; it is, after all, consonant with what we already know about the nature of adult learning.

The Context of Learning

Until recently, theory building in adult learning was approached from a psychological perspective, that is, the individual learner was the focus. Chapters Eight and Nine present two perspectives that take as their starting point the larger society in which the adult learner lives.

As Welton reviews in Chapter Eight, critical theory, via its primary spokesperson, Habermas, posits that the human being has the capacity to learn and, in particular, to be a reflective, critical learner; however, the social structures, the institutions, the conditions of people's lives often prevent them from developing individually and collectively. In addition, the notions from critical theory that there are possibly three types of knowledge (technical, practical, and emancipatory), that there are ways to think about institutions and society, and that there are ways to communicate more effectively with each other are being taken into consideration as the field of adult education grapples with what it wants to become. The strength of critical theory is that it is challenging adult educators to think more broadly and more critically about practice and about learning in particular.

Feminist pedagogy is another orientation that is helping to inform our understanding of learning from a social rather than a psychological perspective. As Tisdell points out in Chapter Nine, there are two primary strands of thinking within the literature. One strand, the liberatory model, focuses on the power relations in society that have resulted in the oppression of women; these same power relations are reproduced in the education system, including adult settings. A second strand, the gender model, posits that women have been socialized to behave as nurturers, as caretakers, as subordinate beings; this behavior is also carried over into educational situations. Both models, but especially the liberatory, situate women learners in a larger social context. Writing and research from both perspectives have addressed implications for teaching and learning in adult classrooms.

Adult Learning Theory: Concluding Thoughts

It would seem that a complete theory of adult learning must take into consideration the learner, the learning process, and the context. As indicated in the review above, the emphasis of each of the perspectives/theories/models varies. No single perspective provides us with a comprehensive picture of adult learning; however, several do consider more than one dimension. In the feminist pedagogy perspective, for example, the gender model is more psychologically or learner-oriented than is the liberatory model. Thus, both the learner and the context are important considerations in feminist pedagogy. So too, while the transformational learning models document the cognitive changes in this kind of learning, development of the individual learner is also considered; and in Freire's pedagogy, the social context of oppression is what gives rise to transformational learning. Similarly with the situated cognition models, while the emphasis is on cognitive problem solving, the process is an interaction among people, ideas, and the immediate social environment. Whatever the emphasis—learner, process, or context—of each of the orientations presented in Chapters Two through Nine, evidence of the other two factors is likely to be present.

Some concluding observations can be made about the state of the art of adult learning theory. First, andragogy, while not a theory of adult learning, does contribute to our understanding of the adult learner. Because of its intuitive validity and because the assumptions underlying andragogy are and have been easily translated into practical guidelines and mandates, andragogy is here to stay. The same can be said about self-directed learning, where we shall see even more exploration and theory building taking place. It is not at all clear, however, how self-directed learning might be worked into a larger, grander theory of adult learning.

Second, consciousness and learning, critical theory, and feminist pedagogy are serving to pry open our thinking about what learning *can* be, what the constraints might be that we have heretofore been unaware, and what the impact on individuals and society might be if we were to free ourselves as learners in the ways suggested by these orientations.

Finally, the research and writing in the areas of transformational learning and situated cognition seem to hold the most potential for moving toward a comprehensive theory of *adult* learning. First, both of these approaches focus on the process of learning, which is consonant with traditional learning theory. In addition, each can accommodate the context of adult life and is perhaps even able to delineate unique features of adult life and thus adult learning. Mezirow, for example, already has proposed that perspective transformation is unique to adults because it requires a certain level of cognitive (and perhaps psychological) development. Likewise, situated cognition posits that learning occurs in "interaction with the setting itself in relation to its social and tool-dependent nature" (Wilson, this volume). One might ask how the social and tool-dependent environment of adults defines the nature of adult learning in contrast to learning in childhood.

In summary, we have come a long way since Thorndike's and others' early investigations of memory, intelligence, and learning. This update on adult learning theory has revealed that there is a growing knowledge base informed by work emanating from adult educators and from practitioners and researchers in other disciplines. What is emerging is a more comprehensive understanding of adult learning, an understanding that is dynamic and that will continue to change as we learn even more about this complex phenomenon.

Reference

Merriam, S. B., and Caffarella, R. S. *Learning in Adulthood: A Comprehensive Guide.* San Francisco: Jossey-Bass, 1991.

SHARAN B. MERRIAM is professor of adult education at the University of Georgia, Athens, and coeditor of Adult Education Quarterly.

INDEX

ORDERING INFORMATION

NEW DIRECTIONS FOR ADULT AND CONTINUING EDUCATION is a series of paperback books that explores issues of common interest to instructors, administrators, counselors, and policy makers in a broad range of adult and continuing education settings—such as colleges and universities, extension programs, businesses, the military, prisons, libraries, and museums. Books in the series are published quarterly in spring, summer, fall, and winter and are available for purchase by subscription as well as by single copy.

SUBSCRIPTIONS for 1993 cost $45.00 for individuals (a savings of 20 percent over single-copy prices) and $60.00 for institutions, agencies, and libraries. Please do not send institutional checks for personal subscriptions. Standing orders are accepted.

SINGLE COPIES cost $14.95 when payment accompanies order. (California, New Jersey, New York, and Washington, D.C., residents please include appropriate sales tax.) Billed orders will be charged postage and handling.

DISCOUNTS FOR QUANTITY ORDERS are available. Please write to the address below for information.

ALL ORDERS must include either the name of an individual or an official purchase order number. Please submit your order as follows:
    Subscriptions: specify series and year subscription is to begin
    Single copies: include individual title code (such as CE1)

MAIL ALL ORDERS TO:
    Jossey-Bass Publishers
    350 Sansome Street
    San Francisco, California 94104

OTHER TITLES AVAILABLE IN THE
NEW DIRECTIONS FOR ADULT AND CONTINUING EDUCATION SERIES
Ralph G. Brockett, Editor-in-Chief
Alan B. Knox, Consulting Editor